free your

creative

Spirit

free your creative Spirit

VIVIANNE AND CHRISTOPHER CROWLEY

WALKING STICK PRESS
Cincinnati, Ohio

First published in Great Britain in 2001

by Godsfield Press Ltd

Godsfield House, Old Alresford

Hampshire SO24 9RQ, UK

First published in North America in 2001

by Walking Stick Press

an imprint of F&W Publications, Inc.

1507 Dana Avenue

Cincinnati, OH 45207

1-800/289-0963

ISBN 1-58297-089-0

2 4 6 8 10 9 7 5 3 1

© 2001 Godsfield Press

Text © 2001 Vivianne and Christopher Crowley

Designed for Godsfield Press by

The Bridgewater Book Company

Studio photography by Mike Hemsley FBIPP at Walter Gardiner Photography

Illustrations by Kim Glass

Cover photo image: Shelly Corbett/FPG International LLC

Vivianne and Christopher Crowley assert the

moral right to be identified as the authors of this work.

Printed and bound in Hong Kong

contents

creation song

Singing the song, I rejoice,

I sing the song of creation,

I sing the stars in their constellations,

I sing the suns that bring forth life,

I sing the moisture and

the rich fertile earth,

I sing the song, I rejoice.

I am singer, a singer of creation,

I am voice, a voice within the void,

I am light, the light unceasing,

I sing the song, I rejoice.

Vivianne Crowley,
St. James's Church,
London, December 2000

Prelude

do you feel that inside you there is a creative person who is struggling to get out? Are you a frustrated writer, dancer, actor, inventor, painter, musician, or innovator? Do you sense that deep within you is a creative urge, but you do not know how to express it or set it free? If so, this book will help you unlock your creative potential and achieve your creative goals.

This book describes a process for freeing your creative spirit, the inner creative you. We believe that all human beings are creators, so becoming creative is a process of unfolding what is latent within you. We can most easily access our creative selves if we embark on a voyage of self-discovery. We can embark on this voyage if we discard the inhibitions and inner barriers that hold us back. We can let go of inner barriers when we have confidence in ourselves. We have confidence in ourselves when we have had positive experiences of manifesting our creativity. This book contains experiential exercises to assist you to do just that—to express your creative potential. The more you learn to access your creativity, the more you will feel empowered. When we feel empowered, we have energy—the energy to begin our creative projects and to see them through until the end. Working on creative projects gives us joy and the desire and motivation to continuing improving what we do. Creativity then becomes a developmental process that helps us change, grow, and become our true selves, that which we were always meant to be.

Creativity

Creativity is an inner state of being. It is fed by sensory experience—sight, sound, smell, taste, and touch—as processed by our brains and stored in our memories. Our imagination harnesses these sensory impressions to create something that is greater than the sum of the parts—a new creative idea. Our skills and training take this idea and express it through a creative medium, such as art,

ABOVE *Leap by leap you will discover your natural inner creativity.*

music, dance, acting, or writing. The result is a creative output. Our creative work produces new sensory inputs and new creative ideas, and practice develops our skills so that our creative work develops, grows, and improves. This book is a starting point on an exciting journey—a journey to help you reclaim your creativity. Step by step—and leap by creative leap—*Free Your Creative Spirit* awakens your inner creative self. You will learn about the sources of creativity in the human psyche, and that creativity is the heritage of us all. You will learn to use words, images, sounds, and ideas to produce creative work that speaks with your voice. School often inhibits our creativity. Education teaches logic and not intuition, control and not spontaneity, perfection and not experimentation. We lose our creative confidence and decide that creativity is something that only special "creative" people possess. In order to release your creativity, you need to undo this negative programming to enable your creative imagination to run free. Creativity is a flame within us— we are all creative. This book is to help you feed that flame.

Creativity is like fire—this is one analogy. Creativity is also like water—a stream that flows with clear, dancing water from the mountain top to join with other streams to form mighty rivers of ideas that fertilize and enrich our world. Creativity is energy. According to Indian religious tradition and the Jewish mystical system of the Kabbala, the whole universe is created from Divine energy. When we act creatively, we stimulate our creativity further.

We remove blockages to the flow of creative thought, so the stream runs faster and the creative flow is swelled. When our creativity flows out into the world, it feeds the creativity of others, and the world is made richer. The world needs your creativity. To make our societies work and to make them joyful, we need the Divine power of creativity to help us produce beauty, ideas, and innovations that can make our societies better places in which to live.

66 A journey of a thousand miles must begin with a single step. 99

LAO-TSU,
Chinese philosopher

rediscovering

Rediscovering

"The important thing is to create. Nothing else matters; creation is all." PABLO PICASSO, *painter*

"I am creative." What does this mean? Does it mean that you can write, draw, paint, decorate a room, carve wood, think of a new product, make clothes, cook, renovate a house, organize a wedding? Does it mean you can keep a class of students engaged in your subject, act, belly dance, tell funny stories about your day at work, think of bedtime stories for your children, devise holidays for friends that you know will be relaxing, stimulating, and fun? The answer, of course, is that all these activities use our creativity. We use our creativity every day of our lives. Some of us do creative work such as painting, writing, singing, acting, or dance, either as a job or leisure pursuit. Others do myriad other activities that call upon our skills of inventiveness and imagination.

We are all creative but most of us are unaware of it. This book is for those who would like to be conscious of their creativity and would like to use it more. Becoming creative means first remembering that we are creative. All children are creative. As children, we draw, paint, dress up, invent plays, make things, and tell stories, just as our ancestors did thousands of years ago. The earliest known expression of human creativity is in beautiful cave paintings more than two million years old.

In our highly sophisticated technological societies, many of us lose touch with our creativity. Until industrialization took over in the 19th century, everyone took part in creative activity. We made our own clothes, often dyeing, spinning, weaving, and knitting the very fabric from which they were made. We made the furniture for our houses. Often people made the houses themselves. If we look at these homespun, homemade, and self-built objects, we see that they have beauty and proportion: our ancestors were possessed of an innate esthetic sense. Today, we no longer make the things that we need in everyday life—they are produced in factories by others. Many everyday artistic activities have been usurped

by technology. Instead of singing songs around a piano, we play a CD. We no longer sew beautiful quilts, we buy one from a store. We no longer paint watercolors of our travels. Instead of a few lovingly rendered and treasured images, we have thousands of photographs taken in a few seconds. Technology is good, but it can be disempowering. Instead of spending our spare time in active creativity, we spend it in passive listening and watching. Owning our creativity means switching from passive to active, from consumer to creator, from audience to actor.

This is a book about finding yourself and releasing your creative potential. It describes a process whereby you can discover the creative you. To discover your creativity, you

ABOVE *Children express their creativity through inventive play activities.*

must begin with yourself—with what is inside you. Firstly, you have to believe you can do it. Beliefs become lodged in our brains from all manner of sources. We have beliefs we were taught as children. They become embedded in our psyches,

LEFT *Early cave art was highly sophisticated and creative.*

rediscovering

unquestioned assumptions that we take for granted. We have beliefs gained from our life experiences. We have beliefs that we have absorbed from people whose judgment we trust—parents, teachers, experts, political and religious leaders, book authors, and figures in the media. Many beliefs are irrational ideas that we have absorbed before we were strong enough or mature enough to question their accuracy. We have all manner of beliefs, but to free our creative spirits we need only one kind. This is self-belief.

You may have tried self-help books to help your personal development. This book is similar in that it is a book to help you to help yourself. It is focused on only one thing—your creative development.

BELOW *We need real self-belief in order to release our creativity.*

Today, there are many excellent self-help books that are based on our growing human knowledge about our own inner psyches and psychological make-up. Some are less helpful. Their approach is like the old trick of looking in the mirror and saying, "Every day in every way, I get better and better." Unfortunately, unless you already have strong self-belief, this approach will not work. Your conscious mind is trying to force your unconscious mind to reinforce ideas it doesn't really believe. So how can we get round this problem?

To release our creative potential we need real self-belief. Our self-belief can be enhanced by positive experiences that demonstrate that we have creative potential. Much of this book is designed to allow you to demonstrate that, yes, you are creative. Sometimes, this is through exercises that encourage you to try creative activities. Other exercises are designed to help you journey in the depths of your psyche to discover that within you is an enormous source of creative energy and ideas. As you start to have positive experiences of creativity, these will undo negative programming due to bad experiences in the past. Bad experiences accumulate when you are told that you are not creative, your talents and abilities are inferior, that only "special" people are creative, and you are not special. Perhaps you were told as a child that creativity is not for "people like us." It's for the rich, the lucky, the incredibly talented, people from a privileged background, people from families of creative people. If we think that only special people can create, we are creating—but only negative beliefs that will inhibit the creative process.

You can undo these bad experiences by creating good experiences that show you that the negative messages are not true. When you have good experiences, you feel empowered. Your confidence soars and you try harder and take greater creative risks. You become less sensitive to criticism and seek out the advice of others without being so overwhelmed by other people's advice that you feel obliged to take it. When you feel empowered, you think that your creative work is worth spending time on. As you spend time on it, you become more skilled and begin to master your chosen medium. When you feel empowered, you have the courage to keep going when the going gets tough; you keep at it and go through the pain barrier that all creative people experience when

ABOVE *The universe is constantly creating new forms and discarding others.*

trying to produce creative work. Creative work is not easy. It involves self-doubt, sometimes even terror. It involves the risk of exposing one's inadequacies—as well as joy, enthusiasm, energy, and enormous personal satisfaction. When we feel empowered, we have the courage to try continuously to improve what we do. When we feel empowered, we become creative. We release our true creative spirits.

Our creative species

We are one of the few conscious species in our universe. When you look out into the universe at night and sees stars, planets, and maybe, if you are really lucky, a comet or shooting star, then you may sense that somewhere out there another conscious being is looking from its planet to ours asking the same question: "Is there life out there in the universe? Are there other conscious beings like me?" As we look out, we have to be aware of something else— that we are rare. Biological life is rare: most planets do not have it. Biological life with the level of consciousness that humankind has achieved is even

LEFT *We can become part of the creative process of the Divine mind.*

universe. We are assisting it to express all the ideas and visions that it can manifest. We become part of the creative process of the Divine mind. Through our senses we translate Divine inspiration, the creative energy of the cosmos, into material forms such as words, music, and images.

From Stone Age to Internet Age

Our species is uniquely equipped to assist in the task. We have acute hearing that is able to discriminate complex musical sounds. We have acute color vision, much more acute than most animals, and we can discriminate hundreds of different colors. Even those who are "color blind" can discriminate an enormous number of different gradations and shades. Our sense of smell is acute, although most of us do not consciously notice it.

We were fortunate to develop a tool that enables us to use implements and materials to create beautiful artefacts. This tool is our hand, with its fully opposable, jointed thumb that can grasp objects and direct them precisely. Our hands, together with our brains, with their language centers, and our visual imagination,

more rare. When we think only of our own planet, we can think our lives insignificant. We feel that we are only one of teeming billions, but, in the wider perspective of the universe that is our planet's home, we are precious, unique, and important. Each of us is something extremely rare: a conscious being with the ability to create.

The universe is in a constant state of creation. It continually creates new forms and discards others. As conscious beings, we share in that creative process. While other species can do so instinctively, we alone on our planet have the power of choice. We can choose to be instruments of the Divine creativity of the universe; we can connect with the creative energy that fires the cosmos. In choosing to express our creativity, we are helping the evolution of the meant that we could use pens and brushes to record our ideas in words and images, and we could use tools to manipulate materials such as clay, wood, wool, and stone to create objects of great beauty.

We began to create in our earliest stages of human development, probably before we had even developed language skills. Some of our earliest creative projects were ritual acts. Even before the development of the Neanderthals, early humans were making symbolic patterns from the skulls of animals. Later we began to paint caves with beautiful and vibrant animal pictures that were so artistically developed that when they were rediscovered in the 19th century, archeologists believed they were hoaxes. They could not imagine that their early ancestors had such creative talents. Our ancestors had an extraordinary esthetic sense and even the simplest household object of wood or bone

might be carved and polished so that it was an object of beauty as well as utility. Creativity is in our blood, bone, and genetic memory. It is the heritage of us all.

Creativity as play

All children are creative, but creativity can be stifled. We are born with the urge to create, but during the process of growing up, our creativity is often suppressed. Most schools treat music and art as slightly frivolous subjects—leisure activities. Unless we are thought highly talented, our creative gifts may seem to have no obvious link with the serious business of life—taking tests, getting academic qualifications, and earning a living. Ironically, we sideline creativity, while at the same time businesses are desperate for creative people with innovating ideas, which they can implement.

To rediscover our creativity and play successfully we need to contact the "child within." For many of us, the last time we played creatively and without the intervention of judgmental adults was when we were very young children. We inhabited a world rich in imagination and teeming with possibilities. Through our creativity, we can re-access this world by allowing the "child within" to come out to play.

We have to allow ourselves to go back in time to see the world afresh.

> 66 The creation of something new is not accomplished by the intellect but by the play instinct acting from inner necessity. 99
>
> CARL GUSTAV JUNG,
> *psychotherapist*

something to try

Awakening your creative childhood self

• Do something just for the fun of it—go for a cycle ride, go horse-riding, play a round of golf, go dancing at a club, go to a park for a day to hike, go swimming. Choose an activity that is energetic, something you do not often do, and something you enjoy.

• Play games—cards, ball games, Frisbee, tennis, or other games that involve interaction with others. Games stimulate our strategic thinking and take us away from the world of work.

• Smile and laugh—being alive is an exciting adventure and being a conscious being is an extraordinary miracle.

• Sit down—do nothing every now and then, and just dream.

We have to forget the negative programming we received as children that taught us we were not creative, and go back to our core selves, the selves that dreamed and told fairy stories, the selves that were full of the wonder of imagination.

When a great psychologist, a great painter, and a great scientist all agree, then we have to sit up and take notice: to recontact our creative selves, we have to play. "Play" is activity that is exciting, stimulating, but does not have an immediate productive end. When we allow ourselves "playtime," we allow our minds to release themselves from worry, stress, and everyday cares, so that they can do what they were designed to do—which is to rove great vistas, to dream, and to generate new connections between ideas that result in creative innovation. Swiss psychologist Carl Jung was founder of the Analytical Psychology movement and one of the world's most famous psychotherapists and thinkers. Distinguished visitors to his lakeside home near Zürich were often shocked to find him on the banks of the lake making mud pies. In late middle age, his play became more advanced. He

started building walls. From walls, he moved on to inscribing beautiful memorial stones. In addition to his main house, Carl Jung also had a holiday home—a converted stone tower. This he kept deliberately primitive with no electricity or running water. Here he liked to cook, and spent hours choosing menus.

Carl Jung gave time to these creative activities because "playtime" was his thinking time. This physical activity, so different from his daily work as a therapist and writer, allowed him to break free of mental constraints and to be illumined by new insights. This worked. As well as being a full-time therapist, parent of five children, and extensive traveler, Carl Jung was an extraordinarily

ABOVE *When we dance, we release our minds from everyday cares.*

prolific writer whose collected works fill 18 weighty tomes. In the next chapter, let us look at what might be inhibiting our creative potential.

remember

• Negative thinking is: only special people are creative. I am not a special person. I am not creative. Forget this.

• Positive thinking is: humans are an extraordinary species with extraordinary talents. Humans are creative, therefore I am creative. Remember this.

• Your inner child holds the key to your creative self: don't be afraid to play. Once you allow your creativity out to play, you will find that you are far more creative than you had ever imagined.

• Give yourself positive experiences of creativity and they will rid you of the memory of bad ones.

releasing

Releasing your creativity

"*If you do not express your own original ideas, if you do not listen to your own being, you will have betrayed yourself. Also, you will have betrayed your community in failing to make your contribution.*"

ROLLO MAY, *psychotherapist*, The Courage to Create

We have described the innate creativity of the universe. We have talked about ourselves, part of this creative cosmos, as being innately creative. We might accept this on a rational level and intuitively we might know this to be true—but how do we access the creativity within us? How do we unlock, or unblock, the innate creativity that lies trapped beneath the surface?

Motivating

It is obvious when we say it, but sometimes we have to remind ourselves of the obvious—to create we have to want to create. We have to want it enough to be willing to input time and energy into the process. We have to be emotionally engaged with the process, to feel that we are expressing something deep and important within us.

We want to create when we enjoy what we have created. When we begin, we have to remind ourselves that at this stage other people's opinions and their judgment of what we do are not important. You are

66 There is nothing greater than the joy of composing something oneself and then listening to it. 99

CLARA SCHUMANN, *composer and pianist*

your first audience. When you begin to create, you are creating for yourself. You are doing it because you want to do it—and you are doing it because it is fun.

Permitting

To devote time to creative expression, we have to give ourselves permission to spend time on an activity that may not make us any money. Initially, pursuing our creativity is likely to cost us money in terms of buying materials and tools, and getting training to develop our skills. To begin, we have to make a contract with ourselves that creative activity is important and it is

ABOVE *Make a contract with yourself that creative activity is important.*

right for us to spend time and money on it. To become creative, we must learn to value ourselves, to think that we are worthwhile spending time on and that what we produce is worthwhile. Many of us think just the opposite, that our time must be given totally to others—work, children, friends, partners, and aging parents. How do we set aside time that is "just for me," time to "be," to dream, imagine, record our thoughts and feelings, and to plan? It is important to think about this because you may have all manner of unconscious barriers that discourage you from spending time on creative activity. Barriers may come from parental or cultural conditioning that decrees you should spend every available working hour in making money or caring for your family. Devoting time to anything else may seem frivolous or irresponsible. If you are a parent, you may feel you should be developing your children's creativity rather than your own. If you are plagued with guilt feelings, remember that your children will copy what you do more than what you say. If you want them to think that creativity is important, then give them the opportunity to see adults being creative.

Letting go of fear

What are you afraid of? This is a question often asked of people about to begin a creative career. There are real fears, such as the fear of poverty: should I really be doing this rather than working on a practical career job that I know will guarantee me an income? There is fear of inadequacy: am I really any good? There are thousands of talented people out there who don't make it, so why should I be different? Are my ideas stupid? Will anyone buy my work? All these worries are pointless. Susan Jeffers wrote a book with a wonderful title, *Feel the Fear and Do it Anyway*. If you want to create, then at some point you have to go for it.

something to try

What am I afraid of?

Creativity can be scary. If we are to create, we must show something of our inner motivations, fantasies, needs, desires, preoccupations. To be truly creative, we have to know our emotional heights and depths; we must know ourselves. To begin our creative journey, we must be willing to explore our deepest feelings. Ask yourself some questions about your inner fears and write down the answers.

• What am I most afraid of finding out about myself?

• What am I most afraid of other people finding out about me— my partner, mother, father, my children, best friend, boss?

• What is my biggest fear about expressing my creativity?

• Whose criticism about my creative efforts would most hurt me— my partner, my mother, my father, my children, my best friend, my boss, my agent, my client, other people in my field? And why?

Here you are looking at your fears, which are part of the dark and hidden side of you. Looking at our fears is not always pleasant. Often we would prefer to ignore them, but, if we do not acknowledge them, they can trip us up. Another plus is that if we get used to examining our fears, we can develop a greater understanding of any characters we create. If you are a writer, photographer, portrait painter, actor, or dancer, each of your characters or subjects will have a dark and hidden side and it is important to think about what this might be. This is your character's weakness and vulnerability, where they will most hurt and where it will be easiest to give them pain. In thinking about our characters' dark sides, we are "fleshing them out" and making them whole. We are helping them to become "real." The more we understand ourselves, the more real our characters will be.

Otherwise, you will feel miserable in later years because life has passed you by and you have never taken the first courageous step toward trying to become what you want to be.

Exposing

If you start your creative work, you have to face another fear—that of showing your inner thoughts, dreams, images, ideas, and exposing them to the scrutiny of others. A common dream is finding ourselves in a social situation and discovering we are completely naked. We are terrified of being found out, of being exposed, as we are, warts and all. If you begin creative work, you are exposing yourself. A secret side of you will be delighted: deep within all of us is a

ABOVE *Children will believe that creativity is important if they see adults being creative.*

secret exhibitionist who craves praise, attention, and admiration. We also have an inner doubter who is convinced that all we're likely to achieve is ridicule. A similar dream to the nudity dream is that we are about to start giving a large public lecture when we realize we have forgotten our notes and have nothing to say. The unconscious fear is, suppose we discover we are not creative? Suppose we really do have nothing to say? All of these fears and dreams will lessen once you begin your creative work.

But I'm not original!

People can sometimes be inhibited from starting creative work because they think that they have to produce something completely new, something no one has ever thought of before. This is not true. Most creative ideas have been explored before. Creative ideas are innovative ideas. Innovation differs from originality. Innovation builds on the known and takes it in new directions. Even the most innovative contemporary novel is building on lessons learned about structure, plot, and character that the

66 One can argue that there is no such thing as a new idea, but being creative is finding the truth and rigor, the essence, the interpretation of what you are trying to work with. 99

DAVID BEATON,
theater director

writer has unconsciously absorbed ever since he or she started reading. Our great novel may be a departure from the norm, but it is a new variation on an old theme rather than something completely new. The first of our prehistoric ancestors who made up a story to lull his or her children to sleep was an original thinker. The first person to think of the novel was an original thinker. The writers who followed were innovators, reworking a form invented by someone else, giving it their unique insights. When you create, you are bringing the innermost essence of yourself to bear on an established art form. Of course, you may think up some totally new form of creative expression—don't let us inhibit you if you have a wonderful and original idea! Conversely, don't let the need to produce a wonderfully original idea inhibit you.

Will I be any good?

If you are ever in despair and find that your creative expression is not doing justice to your original vision, you are not alone. Alberto Giacometti became a world-famous sculptor whose creations sell for six-figure

BELOW *Refuse to let negative feelings interfere with your creativity.*

sums—but he was never satisfied with what he did. Often creative people are perfectionists. Their output is never as good as the original idea and they suffer from constant self-doubt and frustration at the inability of the material form to express the full essence of their inner vision. This may not be true of you. You may be one of those fortunate people who has a vision and is so swept up in it that there is never any room for doubt. As you become accomplished in your chosen medium, this may become true for you, even if it wasn't so at the beginning. It is unlikely to be true at first. Often we

ABOVE *If we burdened ourselves with the notion that everything should be perfect, we would never succeed.*

are own worst critics. We judge ourselves too harshly and in doing so abandon our attempts too easily. To learn, it is necessary to fail some of the time. If we never failed, if we were perfect at everything first time, there would be little point in attempting anything. We can, however, circumvent the negative inner critic that is never satisfied by our creative efforts by rethinking how we look at creative activity. Regarding it as "work" is an invitation for the judgmental adult that is a part of all of us to review, appraise, and be critical of all that we attempt. How can we fail to be discouraged under this constant, undermining pressure? When we begin, we needn't think of creative projects as work. They are simply "play." We will make mistakes while we are following our creative path. Not everything will be perfect, but imperfect works are opportunities to learn what works and what does not. We are conditioned by life to think that a mistake is an indication of inadequacy, but it is no such thing. It is simply an experiment that didn't work, one that we can learn from.

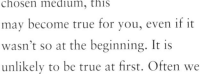

66 If I could make a sculpture or a painting (but I'm not sure I want to) in just the way I'd like to, they would have been made long since (but I am incapable of saying what I want). Oh, I see a marvelous and brilliant painting, but I didn't do it. I don't see my sculpture, I see blackness. 99

ALBERTO GIACOMETTI, *sculptor*

We are usually our worst critics and our most misleading. We have talked earlier about the part of ourselves—the judgmental adult persona—which inhibits our creativity. It is the insidious tempter that whispers you will never be good enough, that people will laugh at your efforts, and slyly suggests that you should be doing something more useful. Ignore these siren voices. Creativity is inspired risk-taking. You have nothing to lose but your inhibitions. I (Vivianne) can always see everything that's wrong with any book I write—but if someone criticizes a book it's never for the reasons I expect. When I (Chris) paint a wall I notice only the tiny blemish, the bit where the paint wasn't so evenly applied. Everyone else sees the overall effect. An important thing to remember when we are doing creative work is that it doesn't have to be perfect. If we put that heavy burden on our shoulders, we will never succeed. Weavers of beautiful Persian rugs always tie one knot incorrectly—because only Allah is perfect. Similarly, with our creative work, we strive to make it the best we can, recognizing that our imagination and the finished outcome will never fully coincide. Isn't it fun though, to see how close you can get?

Learn to be patient with yourself. Great writers or artists are not made overnight. This is not the stage to make comparisons with others. The natural tendency, especially when seeking inspiration, is to look at what

chapter 2

BELOW *When you begin your creative projects, think of them as "play."*

others are doing. People who want to be successful writers read novels for inspiration, those who want to paint look at pictures by famous artists in their local art gallery, and so on. This is fine when you are at a stage where you can dispassionately study technique. It is not so good if the excellence of those examples inhibits your personal development. At this stage of your reawakening creativity, it is better to suspend exploration of the techniques and just let the "child within" enjoy the experience of the new medium. Studying technique can come later. Should you seek inspiration, try exploring a different area of creative work. If you wish to paint, paint while listening to music. If you want to write, look at paintings, and so on. Let your unconscious mind absorb the messages of that medium and see how it can be transmuted into your own. At this stage, we are exploring possibilities. Let the inner voice of criticism and comparison be silent. Just enjoy.

Here we have an exercise in storytelling. Regardless of whether you are a budding artist or writer, your work will tell stories. Begin to explore your storytelling gift.

Narrating your story

One of humankind's earliest creative endeavors was to tell stories. We can all tell stories, we do it all the time.

The story that we tell the most is our own story. Most days you are likely to tell someone about something that has happened to you. Your words re-create the scene for your listener and convey your role in the drama. Often as you are describing the incident, you are aware that you are giving a particular slant to the story. You are exaggerating slightly, you are making it funnier, you may even be fabricating whole episodes just to liven it up a little. You are making your role a bit bigger or more important than it is; or conversely, if it isn't a story that shows you in a good light, you are busy minimizing your role and responsibility.

If you want to write, you have a whole wealth of material at your disposal—your own life experiences. Telling your own story is a good way of learning to create a narrative. Start by writing the story of the first years of your life. You might find it helpful to close your eyes and visualize some scenes. Start right at the beginning—you are struggling your way out of the womb. You emerge—where, who is there, what is the atmosphere? Are you loved, wanted, and awaited—or an intrusion, a mistake? What are your first actions, what smells are you aware of, what do you hear, taste, and see? Describe your first hour of life, your entry into the world.

Move forward in time. You are trying to walk. Who is there? Are they helping or hindering you? What are your emotional reactions to the tricky business of becoming a biped? Is it exciting, dangerous, frustrating, funny? Where are you? What is there around you to explore? What do your fingers grab hold of? What do you stick in your mouth?

Move forward again. Go to an early memory of playing with a friend. Describe your friend. What are you doing together? What are you saying to one another? What emotions do you feel? Are you playing happily? Are there any adults around and are they pleased by what you are doing? Are there tensions, rivalries? Do you get into trouble?

Move forward to your very first day at school. You are getting ready to go. Who is helping you? What are you wearing? Are you worried—and what are you worried about? Are you excited—what are you excited about?

In describing these scenes, you are attempting to encapsulate episodes of your life in words. You are using words to describe what you see, hear, feel, and maybe taste and smell. You are re-creating an experience so that someone else can enter into that experience. In effect, you are giving someone else a window into your private world. Supposing that instead of using words to describe these scenes, you were to paint them. Where would you freeze the frame? What five images would represent these five episodes of your life? When

BELOW *Your own life experiences provide you with a wealth of story material.*

remember

....

• You are unique: there is no one the same as you. No one else has the same experiences and memories.

• You have something to say and you want to find out what it is. You are working on finding out how to say it.

• Give yourself permission to be creative: it's time well spent.

• Don't be afraid: it's OK to make mistakes.

• Silence the inner critic and just enjoy.

you move into the visual mode combined with the verbal one, you are moving into a different form of writing—that of the play or the film or television screenplay. If you discard the words entirely and want to convey the episodes purely visually, you are moving forward again, this time into art. In whichever medium we choose, we are performing the creator's task. We are creating another reality in such a way that other people can expand their personal experience by stepping into it.

Our life stories are the sum total of our experiences made into narrative forms. To have materials to produce our creative work, we must have sensory experiences that stimulate our creative imaginations. Let us now journey into the sensory world.

LEFT *Your life story is a narrative made up of your own unique experiences.*

experiencing

Experiencing

"Learn to see, and then you'll know there is no end to the new worlds of our vision."

CARLOS CASTANEDA, *anthropologist*

Being creative involves communicating sensory impressions combined with the working of our imaginations through an expressive medium, such as art, language, music, or body movement. To become creative we have to start to notice the world around us. Most humans are born with the same set of sensory tools, but each of us will find that some sensory modalities work better for us than others. Our sensory acuity will influence what information we gather, the way in which we process information, and the way we find it easiest to communicate creative ideas. Some people learn best through aural presentation. They need to hear someone describe something for it to come alive. If they read about it, they cannot absorb its essence. If you prefer to have something explained by a trainer rather than teaching yourself from a book, then the auditory world of speech is likely to be an important mode of expression for you. If you

want to write nonfiction, you may find it easier to imagine that you are talking to an audience. If you are writing fiction, you may want to convey most of the story through dialog rather than description. There are tools that can help you. Famous British romance novelist Barbara Cartland, step-grandmother of the late Princess of Wales, wrote hundreds of novels—except that she didn't physically write at all. She dictated all her novels to a secretary. You are unlikely to be able to afford a secretary, but you may well be able to afford voice-activated software for your computer. You can sit in the privacy of your room, headphones on and microphone at the ready to dictate the blockbusting novel or screenplay of the century.

Other people learn best from what they can touch and handle. Their primary modality is tactile and kinesthetic. They enjoy manipulating materials with their hands. Sculpting,

pottery, craftwork, and many forms of art are ideal media if touch is an important part of your repertoire. Many people who are highly tactile find that their visual memory of objects works best when they have handled something. Similarly, word descriptions can spring from memories of touch—the sensual touch of a sexual relationship, the smooth velvet of a cat's fur, the cold, damp stone of a prison wall, the sharpness of the spikes of a holly leaf. If you are tactile and want to write, start with what you can appreciate better than others—the tactile world.

If you are visually oriented, you will learn from what you can see. You may have artistic ability that can work using visual images, or it may

ABOVE *Travel writer Tim Cahill takes time to write in British Columbia.*

be that you are visual but are oriented toward processing words—you need to read something to learn about it. If you are a visual person, but seem to have no artistic talent, this doesn't mean you can't use your highly developed visual sense. Writing takes many forms. If you compare a number of novels, you will find that some writers produce brilliant dialog and their story line is conveyed primarily through the characters' spoken interaction. Others focus on visual description, and environments that we have never seen are created in our imaginations by the images that their words evoke. If you are kinesthetic, and touch and physical movement are the most salient sensory modalities for you, you will find that you can understand your own emotions best by how they register in your body. If you want to write, get used to noticing your physical reactions to different emotional situations and let these be one of your starting points for writing. Describe body movements and what it is to touch and be touched. If you are a "foodie" with gourmet leanings, a wine connoisseur, a lover of fine coffees and teas, learn to describe in words the different tastes that you love and your feelings about them. If you have a strong awareness of smell, notice the smells of different environments—a school, a home, a sports stadium, a city street,

BELOW *Each of us responds to any sensory stimulus in a unique way.*

a bank, a courtroom, a store, a theater. Go along to these places on a smell investigation and note down what you find. For those who do not share your sensory specialization, you will open up worlds that they might otherwise never access or imagine even existed.

Nurturing

Our brains are sophisticated systems that process complex intellectual and emotional information, while at the same time running the complex system of the body. Our brains need feeding in that they need good physical nutrition if they are to function well. They are also hungry for sensory stimulation. They need mind food as well as physical food. Different sensory modalities need different stimuli. We need music and language to stimulate our hearing. Our vision needs images. Our bodies need touch.

Smell and taste provide us with extra dimensions to our experiences that can trigger deep emotional responses, as well as a range of immediate reactions from pleasant to unpleasant, ecstatic to disgusted.

Our physical bodies separate out different stimuli as sound or vision, but within our brains where the stimuli are processed, they do not remain pure stimuli. Our memories store information, but information links with other information. Sounds may for us be associated with particular colors, colors with emotions, emotions with memories, memories with particular tastes or smells. Each of us processes any stimulus in a unique way based on our individual physiology, personality, and experience, so each of us will produce creative work that is unique.

Many painters "hear" colors and musicians "see" sounds. Wassily Kandinsky was a Russian painter famous for his abstract art, but his first love was music. He learned the piano and cello at an early age. Like many creative people, he was multi-talented. This can make it difficult for people to find their direction. Kandinsky did not discover that his vocation was to be a painter until he was 29. He studied law and economics at the University of Moscow and then became a successful professor in the law faculty, but his mind was constantly drawn to the wider universe. He wrote about spirituality and this could have been his main focus were it not for visiting an exhibition of the new painting that was beginning to influence Europe—Impressionism. At first, the style puzzled and frustrated him. He saw Claude Monet's painting *Haystacks at Giverny* and had to look in the catalog to see what it was. The lawyer in him was upset that anyone could paint in such an imprecise fashion, but the exhibition was a staging post on what was becoming an inner journey to change his life direction. Soon after the exhibition, Wassily Kandinsky decided that he must study art and went to Munich to study life drawing, sketching, and anatomy. His early training as a musician influenced his education as an artist. First, he would learn technique, then he would learn to improvize. What had frustrated him about the Impressionists began to influence his own art. Colors began to "sing" for him and he wanted to achieve the same intensity of experience with color as he did with music. He applied them with emotional intensity—streaks and blobs of color were plastered on to the canvas with a palette knife. Kandinsky, who was shocked at Monet, became a founding father of abstract art, often finding himself at the center of controversy

Color is life;

for a world without colors appears to us as dead...

Coloring

As flame begets light,

so light engenders colors.

Colors are the children of light, and light is their mother.

Light, that first phenomenon of the world,

reveals to us the spirit and living soul of the world

through colors.

JOHANNES ITTEN, *painter*

among the public, art critics, and his artistic contemporaries. The musical experiences of his youth never left him as a painter—paintings appeared with names such as *Improvizations*, *Impressions*, and *Compositions*.

Coloring

For Kandinsky color was sound, for his teacher, Itten, it was light. When we see color, we are seeing light reflected on different surfaces, which send different stimuli to our optical apparatus of eye and brain. We marvel at the rainbow because, due to refraction, light has been split so that we are seeing all the colors that it can make. We think of the rainbow as having seven colors because we can most easily discriminate between these seven but, as one shade fades into another, there are scores more to be seen. The next time you have the opportunity to look at a rainbow, see how many colors you can discern other than the standard red, orange, yellow, green, blue, indigo, and violet. Look at where green fades to blue and creates turquoise. What about the tangerine between orange and yellow, and the lime between green and yellow? These subsidiary shades are less intense, so we are less likely to notice them, but they are there.

Color fascinates us because it has a strong emotional impact. Certain colors depress us; others energize or soothe us. Color theory in art was developed primarily through the work of Swiss painter Johannes Itten. Itten headed his own art school in Vienna before joining the Bauhaus from 1919–23, the famous modern art school movement banned by Adolf Hitler in 1933 as subversive. Totalitarian regimes are never keen on creativity—it opens people's minds. At the Bauhaus, Itten designed an

BELOW *Learn to work with light and color to create abstract art.*

innovative training that emphasized stimulating creativity by the unusual usage of common materials. Students were given wire mesh, cardboard, newspapers, gramophone needles, matchboxes, and razor blades, and told to "*basteln*," that is, create something. Johannes Itten also wanted his students to expand their sensory awareness. They were encouraged to touch and draw wood, feathers, mosses, and leather hides until they knew them by heart and could draw them from memory. Itten also asked his students to explore form, color, rhythm, and contrast, in order that they transcend realistic reproduction to achieve an interpretative design rather than an

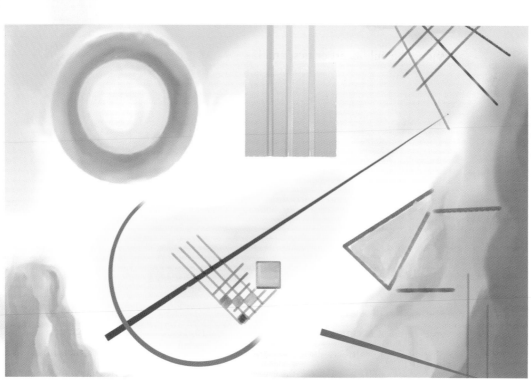

ABOVE *Experiment with paint to develop your color sensitivity.*

imitation of life. Itten influenced modern art innovators such as Wassily Kandinsky and Paul Klee.

As well as stimulating creativity, Joseph Itten was the most famous color theorist of the 20th century. Itten's color wheel is a circle divided into six equal segments. The three primary colors of red, blue, and yellow are separated by three secondary colors formed by mixing two of the primaries, so the sequence is red, purple, blue, green, yellow, orange—and back to red. The primary and secondary colors that appear opposite one another in Itten's color wheel—blue and orange, yellow and purple, red and green—are complementary colors. All colors travel in waves within light, and color complements have different wavelengths. Cones within the eye

detect color and rods detect brightness and dark. If we place complementary colors too close to one another, they cause perception problems. There is too much information for the rods and cones of the eye to handle and we may see a quivering or optical distortion. When using the colors together we also need to be aware of ratios. Itten's theory was that for harmonious balance, colors needed to be used in different proportions. Orange is much more intense that blue, so a ratio of 5:3 in terms of blue to orange works well. Similarly, yellow is more intense than violet so 6:1 works well with violet to yellow. When the three primaries are put together, yellow has greater luminosity than red or blue, so the most harmonious proportions of the primary colors are 3 yellow: 6 red: 8 blue. Once you become aware of Itten's color theory, you will notice that these color ratios are used in everything from office design, to airport lounges, to clothing, to tableware, to abstract paintings.

Learning to work with light and color to create abstract art can free us from the burden of believing that we can only be artists if we can do representational drawing. This does not mean that technical skills such as drawing and learning about perspective and other "tricks" that help the eye to see a two-dimensional line drawing as a three-dimensional object are not important, but they can prove a block to people to whom this does not come naturally. I (Vivianne) draw very badly, but I once won first prize in an art competition, not a major competition, it's true, but a first prize that was a complete surprise to me, because I allowed my imagination to run free with color.

Increasing your color awareness

Develop your color sensitivity by experimenting with paint. Regardless of whether you want to be a creative artist, writer, dancer, or other performer, painting can be a way of stimulating your creative imagination. Buy a selection of paints and some art paper and try experimenting with abstract painting. Take a walk in your local neighborhood. Pick two colors that you like and notice how many times you see them along the way.

Experiencing new stimuli

Stimulating our vision through color is one way of increasing our visual awareness; another way is to step out of our familiar environments to explore new ones. An old cliché is that travel broadens the mind. This is self-evidently true. When we go to a new environment, we look, hear, smell, and taste a realm of new sensory input. We unconsciously compare and contrast the novel environment with the memory of the old, familiar world we have left behind. We learn about new people, buildings, landscape, music, food, clothing—all the different cultural, biological, and geographical aspects

BELOW *Don't let poor drawing skills stop you believing in your artistic ability.*

of the region we visit. A new environment exposes us to new ideas, new modes of thought, and new life experiences. All this sensory experience is food for our hungry creative brains. Travel also helps us in another way. When we re-enter our everyday world, we have new insights and perspectives on it. We notice anew what we had ceased to notice. We see the colors, notice the smells, and are aware of the environment of our home surroundings in a way that we would not have been if we had not stepped outside them for a while.

One important thing to remember about creativity is that it involves processing sensory information. We may be better skilled in one sensory modality than others. Maybe we have refined hearing that makes us good at sound discrimination and we are drawn to music for our creative expression. Perhaps we have insight into how to represent what we see in the world around us using paint or another art medium. Perhaps we can paint a "picture" using words so that someone else can see the people and scenes that we have described. Our medium of expression becomes writing. This does not mean that our creativity will be fed only by exposure to the modality in which we work. If we want to be good writers, then reading other people's work is a good starting point, but at some point we

have to stop reading the "voice" of other writers and find our own. At this point, it can help to stimulate our creativity if we expose ourselves to other modalities and sensory experience. Creating artwork and listening to classical music will stimulate creative thoughts that will result in writing ideas. If you are artistic, reading books and listening to music will help you think of new directions and subject matter for your art. Musicians are often stimulated by looking at art and by "natural art"— the natural world around us. Walking in beautiful countryside is a wonderful way of stimulating our creativity. Exposing ourselves to the sights, sounds, and smells of nature, and

BELOW *Traveling exposes us to new ideas, modes of thought, and life experiences.*

occupying our bodies with exercise, all help free our minds from their usual thought patterns and make the psyche receptive to new creative ideas.

Registering your environment

Travel is a stimulus to our creativity, but we can also get stimulation from our home environment. Start to see your neighborhood in a new light by getting under the surface. Set aside a day to visit a place or attraction in your locality that you have never visited, or go to an event that you have never attended before. You can often identify possible events by reading local newspapers. Some events may be of enormous importance to sectors of your community. It might be a political meeting, a religious service, a school, an artistic, or sports event. Go with your notebook or sketch pad, or take a camera.

Ask yourself questions. What kind of people are there? How many men and how many women? What social, racial, and age groups? How do the people interact with one another? What is the emotional atmosphere? Is there anything going on beneath the surface? Are they there for the primary purpose of the event or to interact with the other people, to be seen to be there, to make their own point, to have a beer? Make notes or sketch. Take photographs, if appropriate, thinking about what moments might most capture the mood. If you are a writer, your sequence of photographs could be the basis of all or part of a story about the event or a similar one.

something to try

Stimulating your sense of smell

What are the tastes of your childhood—milk shake, cola, fries, a particular ice cream? Shut your eyes and imagine the taste of a favorite childhood food, perhaps one that you no longer like now. Remember a time when you tasted it. Where are you? Who is there? Is it a good time or a bad time in your life? What emotions, scenes, sounds, sensations, and people does the taste recall for you?

Stimulate your sense of smell by experimenting with essential oils. These can be bought from health food stores or from stores selling natural bath products. They can be added to bath water or burned on a perfumed oil burner, and some can be used as massage oils. Different oils produce different psychological and emotional reactions. Here are some traditional associations between oils and the qualities and responses they invoke in us.

Camphor	Intuition
Frankincense	Blessings, purification, healing
Honeysuckle or rosemary	Memory
Jasmine	Relaxation and sleep
Lavender	Clarity of mind
Rose	Harmony, peace, love

Seeing anew

Do you really see your everyday environment—or has it become so familiar to you that you no longer notice what is around you? Take a 10-minute walk along a route that you know so well that normally you walk it automatically, without noticing where you are. When you get home, write down everything that you noticed—the weather, the surface you were walking on, the buildings that you passed, the people you saw.

Smelling

One of the most underrated and vivid tools of our sensory apparatus is our sense of smell. Smells form a background to our emotional life and trigger memories and all manner of unconscious associations. Hospitals often use smells to try to awaken people from coma. When we are first born, our eyes cannot focus well and many of the sounds that surround us are meaningless. We can recognize the emotions conveyed by the noises that our parents make at us, but we do not understand language. It is only gradually that the world of vision and sound begins to make sense. Smell and touch are our most basic and biological of sensory modalities. Animal parents and offspring recognize each other by smell as well as from distinctive cries. A ewe can be fooled into thinking that an orphaned lamb is hers if it is wrapped in the fleece of one of her own dead lambs.

When we lived closer to the natural world, we had to be aware of smell to know who was giving off friendly signals and who was working up for a fight. We had to be able to smell prey and predators on the wind. We had to know when members of the opposite sex were emitting the pheromones that meant they were ready to mate. If you have ever taken a dog for a walk, you will know that your dog is sensing a whole world that you are scarcely registering at all. He or she will know what other animals have passed and their state of health and aggressive, passive, or sexual intentions. Animals can smell the sweat and pheromones left by fear, so if an accident or violent incident has occurred your pet will know and may react accordingly. We

are largely oblivious to this world on a conscious level, but we can absorb it unconsciously. We will often have strange reactions, positive or negative, toward people we hardly know because of the smell signals they are emitting. If you read successful novels, you will find that many writers help to lead us into the imaginary world they are creating by describing smell and that closely related sense, taste. The famous 19th-century novelist Proust wrote a 13-volume novel called *À La Recherche du Temps Perdu*, often translated as *Remembrance of Things Past*, considered by many to be one of the major achievements of 20th-century literature. In one famous scene, the hero Swann is transported

BELOW *Along with touch, smell is the most basic and biological of our senses.*

experiencing

back to his childhood by dipping a French breakfast cake, a madeleine, into his coffee. The years are stripped away and he is once more in touch with his childhood memories.

Listening

Music stimulates our creativity. It also helps develop the brain. Plants grow better, cows milk better, and children grow more intelligent if stimulated by classical music. In a study, one group of three-year-olds studied the piano and sang in chorus every day and the other group did not. After eight months, the musical three-year-olds scored 80 percent higher than the nonmusical group on tests of spatial intelligence, which are indicative of our ability to visualize the world accurately. Spatial intelligence is a highly important skill in the study of

BELOW *Listening to classical music stimulates creativity and intelligence.*

art, design, engineering, and math, as well as for music.

Look in the box on p. 49 for the pieces of music to play. Find some time when you can be alone and play the music in a darkened room. Close your eyes and visualize the context in which the music was made. We'll start with the end of the 19th century and go back in time. Dvorak's Symphony No. 9 in E minor "From the New World" was first performed in the United States in 1893. Antonin Dvorak began writing the music shortly after he first arrived in what for him was a "new world." He had traveled from conventional European bourgeois "old world" Czech society, then under the domination of the Austro-Hungarian Empire, with its royal court living in a fairytale glitter of pomp, jewels, medals, and archaic ceremony, to a country at the forefront of the changes that were to propel us into the 20th century. Dvorak was extraordinarily forward-thinking for the time: "The future music of this country must be founded upon what are called the Negro melodies," he told the *New York Herald*. He also incorporated Native American themes into some of his music.

Imagine you are in the audience at this exciting

listening to music

Hearing the creative voice

Obtain copies of these four pieces of music. They are all considered excellent examples of their era. They may not be musical works that you would normally listen to, but you can stimulate your creativity by taking your sensory experience into new avenues. If you do not want to buy the music, you may find that friends, relatives, or your local libraries have copies.

• Dvorak's Symphony No. 9 in E Minor "From the New World."

• Grieg's Peer Gynt Suite No.2—"Solveig's Song."

• Beethoven's "Choral" Symphony No. 9 in D Minor—the fourth and final section containing "Ode to Joy." The singing starts about 7.5 minutes into the section. Just when you think the singing has stopped it starts revving up again and Beethoven's off for the final round of the first verse.

• Hildegard von Bingen—any of her music, but "O Viridissima Virga" ("O Most Verdant Virgin") is particularly beautiful.

first performance. The New York audience at the symphony's première becomes wild with excitement. As yet few symphonies at all have been premièred in your country, so the event is unusual and exciting. Everyone is in evening dress. Outside, the horse-drawn carriages are waiting to drop the occupants outside the steps of the concert hall. The final arrivals take their seats. The concert hall lights are dimmed and the music begins. You do not fully understand what you are hearing, but you sense in the music a spirit of reaching out to all your country's citizens to draw them together into the new America.

Peer Gynt is a play by 19th-century Norwegian playwright Henrik Ibsen. It is based on a Norwegian folk legend, which is full of trolls, dwarves, and other mythological beings. As one of Norway's leading composers, Edvard Grieg was asked to compose the music. Solveig loves the faithless Peer Gynt, but he betrays her and elopes with another man's wife. Peer Gynt abandons his mistress and wanders the world, having many adventures, but remaining unhappy. Solveig never waivers in her love for him, and after many years of lonely waiting, her patience is rewarded. A repentant Peer Gynt returns to her and she redeems him by her love. Norway is a mountainous country with most of its settlements by the sea. Spectacular mountains and deep sea fjords make up the coastal landscape. Play "Solveig's Song" and imagine her standing, a tall, proud, beautiful, blonde-haired Norwegian woman in a long skirt, a shawl wrapped around her, looking out to sea, awaiting her lover's return.

ABOVE *Norway's mountains and fiords are the setting for "Solveig's Song."*

It is 1824. Beethoven's Symphony No. 9 was written in the last years of his life. The German composer was almost completely deaf. His personal life was lonely and sad, but it was a time of great optimism in continental Europe, a time of increasing democracy, political reform, prosperity, industrialization, and enthusiasm. Imagine you are at the first performance of the symphony, which you know might be the great composer's last. He is at the front trying to conduct, but cannot hear the music well enough to keep time and the orchestra is tactfully ignoring him.

What does the auditorium look and smell like? What would you be wearing? Imagine how the clothes might feel on your body. Who are you attending the performance with? What might the emotional mood of the audience be?

Play the music of the Abbess Hildegard von Bingen and picture the context. It is the 12th century. She is the abbess of the leading women's religious establishment in Germany—the only one, in fact, that is self-governing and not the subsidiary of a male-run monastery. The Abbess is a famous writer, poetess, doctor, preacher, and botanist, as well as a composer of beautiful music. She is 60 years old and in the prime of her creative life. She has been a nun for nearly 50 years and will live 21 years more. She wants her nuns to have music that uplifts them into unity with the Divine. Imagine yourself in the candlelit and incense-filled chapel. The ethereal voices of the nuns are resonating back from the vaulted ceiling. Candlelight reflects from the gold vases of flowers on the altar and from the face of the crucified Christ hanging above. What might your emotions be as you participate in the scene? Imagine the mixed smell of incense, flowers, and the faint smell of sweat from an era in which full washing of the body was a rarity.

When we bring our imagination to interact with music in this way, we are allowing the music to create images and emotions, even smells and tastes, which give it context and meaning and enrich our understanding and enjoyment of it. Similarly, we can understand a painting much better if we think about who painted it, what the painter would have looked like, what he might have worn, where he would have painted it, the landscape or cityscape that would have surrounded him, the political climate of the time—whether it was peace, uncertainty, or war. We begin to enter a little into the mind of the person who created the work and share his or her vision. When we begin to imagine the context of a work, we are moving away from direct sensory experience to the world of the imagination. Let us now step into the imaginary world.

remember

• Our brains are hungry for stimulation: give them mind food—new sights, color, music, smells, and tastes to extend their sensory library of memories.

• Play around a little with the different ways of exploring and expressing your creativity and see where you feel stronger, which one is more "you."

• We can stimulate our creative modality by giving our brains sensory experience from a different modality: the sights of nature or great art will inspire music, music will inspire writing and art, reading will produce images that can be the basis for artwork.

• Use your imagination and knowledge when looking at artwork or listening to music. Find out about the creator of the work and the context in which he or she was working.

• Enjoy developing an appreciation of touch, smell, and taste, as well as an awareness of vision and sound. Use these additional dimensions to make what you describe more "real."

imagining

Imagining

"Imagination is the beginning of creation. We imagine what we desire; we will what we imagine; and at last we create what we will." GEORGE BERNARD SHAW, *playwright*

Many writers start life as great readers. As children, they loved books, partly from a love of the power of words, partly for escapism. For many writers, the real world is painful, difficult, and too intense, so they retreat into a fantasy world. Writers sometimes feel too much and for children with literary gifts, books may be a way out of an environment in which they feel ill at ease. Reading can imbue us with the love of books and the printed word, but reading is a passive activity. When we read, we are feeding on other people's creativity. We escape into a world that they have created for us. In order to become writers, we must create a world for others to escape into. It has to be a world that is so real, so beguiling, intriguing, or in some way fascinating that people want to share it with us. It speaks to them and they respond.

From "such stuff as dreams are made of" our imagination grows and develops, our creativity is given life, and there it is nurtured; but the fantasy world can be a seductive place in which to lose oneself. Most creative people have a secret world, a world of imagination and fantasy. It is a place where imagination, the source of our creativity, rules. Fantasy can be a waking dreamworld we go to when seeking refuge from reality. Sometimes it is an escape to a sanctuary because our external lives are unremittingly grim. Sometimes our fantasies are an escape from the monotony or mundane

66 When I examine myself and my methods of thought, I come to the conclusion that the gift of fantasy has meant more to me than my talent for absorbing positive knowledge. 99

ALBERT EINSTEIN, *quantum physicist*

reality of everyday life, the seemingly endless boredom of a job that does not stretch us, or an escape from a sense of loneliness and alienation. In this world of imagination, we can be things we are not in reality. We can be heroes or great lovers. We can be whoever we want to be; after all, it is our own world and in this one we get to call the shots.

Whether it is good or bad to fantasize depends on whether it is kept in perspective. If it becomes an obsessive pursuit then it is not so good. In excess, instead of stimulating creativity, fantasy saps it. It becomes like a black hole into which all one's creative energy is poured, never to be utilized or, for that matter, ever seen again. It is then a substitute, an ersatz replacement for living your real life and manifesting your creativity. If it is a healthy fantasy world then the opposite may be true. Fantasy becomes a vessel for the creative imagination, almost a bubbling over of ideas and images that, if articulated, can provide a rich source of material for your outward creative expression.

BELOW *Your fantasy world can provide a rich source of inspiration.*

An overactive imagination can be a driving force that leaves us no option but to create. Many famous artists, writers, and musicians were people who had no choice but to create or descend into madness. If you are prone to negative fantasies, anxieties, and nameless fears, it may be because your life is unusually difficult and unstable, or it may be that you have a highly active imagination. If as a child your sensitivity and imagination were not channeled in positive directions, you may be left with a negative fantasy life that makes you preoccupied with negative emotions such as guilt. If this sounds like you, finding a positive outlet for your imagination can transform your life. Art therapy can work wonders because it gives people who have not been able to express themselves a way of giving vent to their innermost experiences and feelings. Art therapy can also work because art can become an energy channel that leaves the mind and spirit exercised in the same way that physical exercise can leave the body and mind in a state of equilibrium and inner peace.

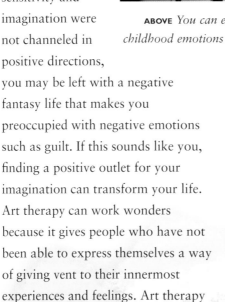

ABOVE *You can express repressed childhood emotions through art therapy.*

Fantasies need not be about fears and anxieties. We have pleasurable fantasies about winning vast amounts of money—the cars, clothes, and other luxuries we would buy and the hedonistic pleasures we could experience from our new wealth. We may fantasize to live out another life. We imagine ourselves in a favorite story or film. We insert ourselves into that scenario, reacting with the various characters so new situations evolve. Alternatively, we may project ourselves into an imaginary world set in the past or future. "What would it be like," we ask ourselves, "if I had the power to heal, to see into the future; if I was sexually irresistible, or a brilliant battle tactician? Suppose I was the ruler of a galactic empire and wielder of strange powers?" The possibilities are endless. Science fiction is fertile ground for this type of fantasy—since it is set in a world beyond reality you can make up all the rules. People whose creative lives are unexpressed can lead exhilarating fantasy lives. People with boring jobs and a rich imagination can have a whole blockbusting fantasy saga in

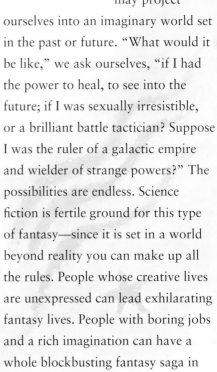

their right brains, while their left, logical brain serves customers, packs on a production line, or cleans floors. Many highly successful novels are based around characters that are "sub-personalities" of the author. Patricia Highsmith, who like many female crime writers had a strong masculine side, lived this out through her "antihero" Ripley, played by Matt Damon in Anthony Minghella's film *The Talented Mr. Ripley*.

Expressing your fantasies

The possibilities of fantasy are limitless. If you have strong fantasies, try drawing or painting some of the characters or writing about them. Follow what we have said about creative writing and suspend all critical, judgmental thought processes. Let the energy of the fantasy pour through your hands on to the paper. Just let it flow. Review what you have created only after a little time has elapsed; enough time to enable you to be slightly detached from your work so you can begin to see it objectively. What have you got? Is it something better kept to yourself? Is it self-indulgence, a private fantasy that captivates you, but would have little interest to others? Even if our fantasies are personal "actings out" of hidden aspects of ourselves, rather than the starting point of a great

novel, expressing them outwardly through writing or art is important.

If you express your fantasies through a creative medium, some of the energy that is bound up in them will be released, and space will be created in your psyche for your true creative work to begin. If you are a prolific fantasist, you may find that once you begin to create you have an outlet for your imagination and your fantasy life goes into abeyance. You have a useful product from your creative imagination rather than sterile fantasy that can become a repetitive form of emotional masturbation. Once expressed and explored, your fantasies will hold less power over you. Often they will not let you go until you have given them

BELOW *Express your fantasies to release the energy to be creative.*

their recognition, their 15 minutes of fame under the spotlight. This will free your creative imagination and let it move on to other things—images, stories, ideas, and plot lines that might be of interest to the wider world.

Having read your fantasy, if you think that you have got something good, you can take it further. If a painting, could it be shown? If a piece of writing, does it read well? If it holds your interest (even when you know the ending!) then perhaps you have something worth publishing. Can you see where it can be improved? Could you develop the other characters, or tighten up the plot? Maybe you will have to allow your wonderful fantasy hero to have just a few more flaws—some of the aspects of yourself that you don't like very much. Can your idea be developed in some way? Is it just an episode or could it be developed into a complete story? If it is a story, could it sustain a series? Can it be converted into a film script or a play? The possibilities are endless and you have done the most important and the most difficult thing. You have made a start—and that is the biggest hurdle out of the way.

ABOVE *A guided fantasy can help you to discover your inner creative self.*

Meeting your creative self

Active imagination is a form of guided fantasy whereby we dialog with our psyches through symbols and images. This is an exercise to help you contact your creative self. This exercise is best done lying down in a warm and comfortable room with dim lighting. You will also need some large sheets of drawing paper and some colored pencils or pens. You should allow about an hour and a half for the exercise. You could read the exercise and visualize each instruction in turn, in which case you may like to write or type the exercise on to a sheet of paper in large print that you can read in dim light. Alternatively, you could read the instructions on to a tape, leaving gaps for the visualization. If you are taping the exercise, leave at least 2–3 minutes between each instruction.

Relax and go within yourself. Let your breathing settle down and let all the busy thoughts of the day drift away. Let yourself sink gently into stillness. When you are ready, you find yourself on a warm summer's day in a beautiful place in nature. The sun

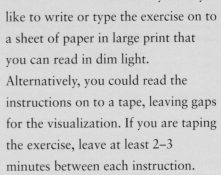

is shining, the birds are singing, and all is warm and at peace. You are at home in this place. You notice that a figure is coming toward you. This is a guide who will take you to a house to meet with your creative self. You find yourself approaching the house. When you are ready, go with your guide to the front door of the house. The guide opens the door and indicates that you can go inside while the guide waits outside. Begin to explore the house. In one of the rooms, your creative self is waiting for you. When you find him or her, sit down and talk. Ask what changes your creative self might need in your life in order to express itself. Are there any internal barriers that you need to work on, to give your creative self the time and space it needs? Ask what your creative self needs of you, and what you can do for it.

When you feel ready, end this conversation, but before bidding your creative self goodbye, ask if there is a symbol he or she would like to give you of your creativity. Now thank your creative self and make your way out of the house. Outside the house, your guide is waiting for you. Thank your guide for assisting you on your journey and in your own time return to your room in the everyday world.

Make the light brighter and, when you feel ready, record your experiences by drawing or writing

them. What was your guide like? Was your guide a person, a spirit, an animal? What qualities did the guide have that you do not possess? Do you need to take on some of these qualities in order to express your creativity? What was the house of your creative self like? Were the rooms empty or full, appropriately or inappropriately furnished? Were any rooms locked? Did you like or dislike the house? What did you like or dislike? Did the inside and outside match? Many people have houses that look insignificant on the outside, but that are sumptuously furnished inside. Are you hiding your inner riches? Some people have grand houses that are unfurnished. Do you need to find skills, ideas, and stimulation to enable you to fill the mansion of your creativity? Are there rooms where the furniture is covered in dustsheets? If so, do these rooms need to be opened? Are there past skills and talents that you have neglected, but should now take up? These skills and talents may not relate directly to your chosen

ABOVE *Let the thoughts of the day drift away.*

something to try

Working through moods and feelings

If you have difficulty interpreting your symbol from your visualization, ask it what it means. Subdue the lighting, play soft music, close the drapes, light a perfumed candle or two. Go back to the moment when your creative self gave you the symbol. Now mentally ask the symbol: what are you for and what do you represent? Ask the symbol to help you to understand it. Notice your feelings—what feelings does your symbol inspire? Sense your mood and flow with the feeling. Where does this take you? Sometimes the mood can be very different from that which the conscious mind might predict. Stay with the mood. When have you had this feeling before? What was happening in your life at that time? Don't give up if the symbol does not give you a response the first time. Instead, notice any dreams that come over the next few days, the answer might lie in them.

creative medium, but they may be ways of facilitating its creative expression.

Was it easy to find your creative self or difficult? Was your creative self near the front door of the house—the threshold between your conscious and unconscious mind? Or was your

RIGHT *Record the experience of your visualization in words or pictures.*

creative self locked away in the basement or living in a lonely attic? What did your creative self look like and what qualities did he or she possess? There will be clues here as to what you need to express your creativity. Did your creative self seem strong or weak, energetic or tired, young or elderly? Was your creative self of the same sex as you or the opposite sex? Our muse may appear to be the opposite sex to ourselves because we need qualities commonly associated with the opposite sex in order to express our creativity. Men who have led very stereotypically masculine lives may need more stillness and calm receptivity if they are to become creative. Women who have been primarily mothers and homemakers may now need to become more self-confident, competitive, and self-focused.

Consider the symbol of your creativity from your visualization. What does it express for you? Is it something that you could make, draw, paint, find, or buy in a store? If you are having difficulty interpreting your symbol, read the box on page 60 to help you.

Mythologizing

Myths are collective fantasies that express the important truths and ideas of a particular culture. Reading stories from myth and fairy tale can be helpful ways of stimulating our creativity. Like Christian parables, myths convey multiple messages that could be understood on many levels. At the simplest level, myths are entertainment. For young children who heard their elders retelling the ancient myths of their people, they would have been exciting bedtime stories. As we got older, we would have understood that there were moral messages in the myths. A little more understanding would have shown us that they conveyed our society's world view and relationship with its gods. We might also have seen another layer of meaning—that the myths conveyed eternal truths about human inner emotional and spiritual life and the processes that accompany psychological growth and change. Mythological stories have archetypal patterns that arise from deep layers of our psyches. One of the ways books and movies have become successful is to adapt these archetypal patterns into stories that appeal to our contemporary imaginations.

George Lucas, the director of the *Star Wars* movies, was advised by Joseph Campbell, a Jungian analyst, author of *The Hero with a Thousand Faces* and an expert on myth. He had explored particularly the myth of the heroic quest undertaken by a young man who seems insignificant, but often is discovered to have royal or other important lineage, and who becomes the hero by destroying the forces of evil. This story is found in all cultures. People all over the world identify with it and people all over the world watched Lucas's films and identified very closely with the myth that was its story line. Myths contain symbols. Sometimes the significance of these symbols is clear and sometimes it is obscure. There are ways of accessing symbols, however, and drawing on their rich meanings.

Symbolizing

Imagination helps our unconscious minds to communicate ideas to our conscious minds. When we imagine we often use symbols. Symbols are a bridge between word and image and are important to writers, artists, and all creative thinkers. To be truly creative, we must be open to a deeper level of consciousness than the average person. At this level, the psyche communicates in symbols.

A symbol is an image that has a special significance. Symbols can be the springboards for advances in scientific knowledge as well as for artistic creativity. Graham Wallas speaks of illumination as the emergence of the "happy idea" that provides release of the tension that has been building through the preparation and incubation stages of creativity. Psychoanalytic writers suggest that this illumination occurs at the level of the unconscious mind. In terms of our cognitive structure analysis, we might say that it does not occur in one's thoughts, but in what one uses to think, the cognitive structures themselves. Perhaps this is the reason that the creative process is not directly accessible to conscious thought and so is perceived to be illogical, mysterious, or unconscious. Friedrich August Kekulé was a German scientist who was descended from Czech nobility. He began his academic studies in architecture. He became fascinated by chemistry when he heard a famous chemist give

> 66 Out of the creative act is born symbols and myths. It brings to our awareness what was previously hidden and points to new life. The experience is one of heightened consciousness—ecstasy. 99
>
> ROLLO MAY,
> *psychotherapist*

forensic evidence at a murder trial. Today, that might seem a good career choice, but in the 19th century, architects were prestigious and influential people who mixed with wealthy patrons. Chemistry was not a promising occupation and his family tried to dissuade him. Kekulé persisted and went on to study for a doctorate. Although he was attracted to chemistry, like many creative people his interests were wide. He enjoyed hiking, debating, learning languages, dancing, juggling, joking, and drawing. He began to make creative breakthroughs when he moved out of his familiar environment and came to work at St. Bartholomew's Hospital in London. He was sitting on a London bus in the days of public transport's infancy when he began to have a waking dream—a kind of vision. The dream had precognitive aspects—it foretold a time when he would be a great chemist:

imagining

ABOVE *Our dreams and fantasies are often full of symbolic images.*

"I had gotten to this point in reviewing my research, when the constant motion of the bus made me drowsy and I drifted into sleep. I found myself dreaming that I was present at the Deutsche Chemische Gesellshaft in Berlin on the occasion of the twenty-fifth anniversary of the Kekulé benzene theory—and I was being given the opportunity to interview the great man! I began to ask him to reflect upon his career since the awarding of his doctorate on June 25, 1852. . . . I saw how, frequently, two smaller atoms united to form a pair: how a larger one

❞ A symbol is an indefinite expression with many meanings, pointing to something not easily defined and therefore not fully known... ❞

CARL GUSTAV JUNG, *psychotherapist*

embraced the two smaller ones; how still larger ones kept hold of three or even four of the smaller: while the whole kept whirling in a giddy dance. I saw how the larger ones formed a chain, dragging the smaller ones after them but only at the ends of the chains.... The cry of the conductor: "Clapham Road," awakened me from my dreaming; but I spent a part of the night in putting on paper... sketches of these dream forms. This was the origin of the Structural Theory."

This was enough to give Kekulé the insights that led to his discovery of the structure of the benzene molecule; for which he is now famed.

A symbol game

Think of five people whom you know and who interact with one another—people you work with, family, or

something to try

See if you can find the following neighborhood symbols:

• A faded advertising hoarding or billboard: what feelings and associations does the scene produce for you?

• An empty house or building: what was its history, its story?

• New roads: what might they bring?

• New people in the neighborhood: what might their life stories be?

Use them as starting points to write a few paragraphs, to photograph, or to draw or paint. You may notice that they have certain commonalties. These objects exist in their own right, but they are also symbols of transition and change. When you are working, contemplate the theme of change—from past to future, new to old—and allow your thoughts and feelings to influence your work.

remember

- Just dream: dreaming allows creativity to take root and grow.

- Connect to your unconscious mind to explore its rich store of myth, fantasy, symbolism, and dream, for that is the most creative part of you.

- Symbols open the door to the collective unconscious: working with symbols will stimulate your creativity.

- Express your fantasies through your creative work, or they will sap your creative energy.

- Properly harnessed, your fantasies can be transformed into creative gold.

chapter 4

friends. Think of some symbols for each of them: what kind of animal, fish, or bird are they? What kind of plant are they? What color would they resonate to and to what kind of music? You can play this game with others. Your children might enjoy it. You will find that there are similarities in the way that a group of people will see others. When you have your set of symbols, choose one person and make a painting or colored drawing incorporating his or her symbols. This need not be an artwork to hang on your wall, but it is a symbolic representation of what your brain has perceived about the person. In modern Western society, our ability to work with symbols is underused and repressed. Our imaginations become rusty with neglect. Getting them working again provides a rich source of sustenance for your creativity. We have stimulated our senses and imagination, now let us move on to apply our developing skills—firstly in the world of light and form.

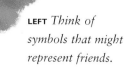

LEFT *Think of symbols that might represent friends.*

envisioning

Envisioning your creativity

"*Painting isn't an esthetic operation; it's a form of magic designed as a mediator between this strange hostile world and us, a way of seizing the power by giving form to our terrors as well as our desires.*"

PABLO PICASSO, *painter*

No matter where we live, whether it is in beautiful countryside or in deprived inner cities, in smart central apartments, in drab countryside, or in either characterful or anonymous suburbs, it is possible to see your environs in a completely new way, in a completely fresh light. "Light" is the key word. Light changes and is always shifting, whether it be through the seasons, in different weather conditions, or at different times of the day. Look at how the light transforms a scene; sometimes in striking, dramatic ways, sometimes more subtly, but always interacting with your surroundings. Take time to observe these changes; connect with them and see how they affect your perception of the scene.

Famous artists from Claude Monet to Nicholas Roerich were drawn back to the same scene to paint it in different lights and all the different aspects that the light created. As well as his famous waterlily paintings and other paintings of his garden at Giverny, near Paris, the 19th-century artist Claude Monet was drawn to the Houses of Parliament on the Thames in London. He painted this scene at dusk, in fog, and in a shimmering industrial sunlight. In a sense, he wasn't painting the subject matter at all; he was painting the light that he saw at different times in the same place. Sometimes the subject matter is clearly delineated; sometimes it is massive, dark, indistinct, and hulking shapes. Sometimes it is bathed in a

golden sunlight, and the dark, brooding shapes of earlier pictures have been transformed into something light, delicate, and ethereal by the golden glow of the sun.

Nicholas Roerich became equally fascinated by this same quality of light, although he chose a very different place to experiment in capturing it. For several years, he lived high up in the Himalayas in order to record the changing light on the mountains around him. The results were stunning. As the clouds swept over the mountain peaks, so shades of green became purple, grays

ABOVE *The quality of light dramatically affects the mood of the scene.*

became blue, new shadows were formed from rocks and crevasses that before had appeared smooth. Moving shadows created jagged dark chasms deeply etched into the mountainside, only to disappear again as the storm clouds moved over and the light shifted once again.

Roerich did not stop at recording the scene. From these paintings, he saw how his mood changed in response to the changing light and the colors that this light generated.

Observing the changing light

Look at the view outside your window seven times during the period of a single day—dawn, midmorning, noon, late afternoon, sunset, twilight, and nighttime. A sunny day is best. Notice the quality of light as it moves

them developed as large prints so you can see the various effects. Polaroids are good for instant results and comparisons, but if using a normal camera it is better not to use one of those "do it all for you" automatic ones that are so good for foolproof snapshots. These will automatically

from a blue note to a golden one and back to blue again. Take a photograph at each stage and have

make adjustments for the light and so your pictures will appear more similar than if you take your pictures on manual or override. What does this sequence of images tell you? How do they affect you? What moods could be generated from each individually and as a sequence, a whole? If writing is your chosen medium, what story could you develop from these pictures? If you want to experiment

ABOVE *Take photographs to compare the changing light through a sunny day.*

with paint, try painting the scenes over a few days, or over different seasons, if you would like to make

this a longer-term project. Try not to make the physical things that you see the focus of the picture—trees, rooftops, brick walls, and windows— but the shapes and colors the light makes on these fixtures in your composition. Work fast for the light will change quickly. Aim for accuracy of color and for the shapes the light makes rather than the details.

This sort of exercise works. By absorbing the visual information, we can feel the effects it has on our moods and emotions and from these we can build our creativity in a different form. It relates back to what we were discussing earlier. If a writer, seek inspiration from the visual; if a painter, seek it from music; if a sculptor, from dance; and so on.

Recording the seasons' change

One of the most striking yet simple sequences of change is of a tree changing through the year's annual cycle. Choose a favorite deciduous tree, one that you can get to easily, and photograph or paint it in each of the four seasons. See it in winter, rooted in the brown earth, skeletal and dormant, bare branches against the cold blue of a winter sky. See it in spring, budding and blossoming, the earth now covered with grass of that fresh, bright green that can only be found in spring. See it in summer at

something to try

Turning photographs into paintings

Another thing that you can do with photographs is to turn them into paintings. You can do this straightforwardly by using a photograph of a scene or person as your subject and painting it, or you can be far more creatively experimental. Take a really bad photograph, the more over or underexposed the better, take it down to your local photocopy store and ask them to photocopy it as enlarged as possible, preferably to poster size.

The larger the photograph gets, the more indistinct—or abstract—the image becomes. The finish will become grainy and, if under-exposed, all the too-dark shadows and bleached areas will take on their own abstract significance. If overexposed, the photograph will take on its own ethereal abstract quality. The original subject matter disappears. See the shape and form of the abstract blocks of light, shadow, and color—you don't even have to keep the copy the right way up. Move it around, look at it from different angles, and see what it suggests to you. Have several copies made, take one at a time and paint over it, accentuating shape, shadow, and form. Give your artistic sense full rein and see what happens. It's exciting to see art emerging in this way. It can convert an indifferent photograph into an exciting piece of art.

its most majestic and glorious in full leaf. See it in the fall, its leaves turning to the riches of copper, red, and amber hues; the earth around it browning again with the grass long, lank, and spent.

In these exercises, we are always looking at the same thing, but by looking we see that it is never the same. It is always changing; it always has something new to tell us, and there is always something new to learn. We can discover all this from one tree, or from one view from a window. No matter where we live or what we do, we can draw on thousands of new sights and visions that feed our creativity each day. It is all in the seeing of things.

ABOVE *Choose a particular scene to watch as it changes through the seasons.*

Sensing the form in things

All of us will have a creative medium that we will relate to more closely than any other. For many it will be writing or the visual arts, but these

LEFT *Capture the beauty of a tree and its summer foliage.*

will not be for all. Many will find music, for example, to be both their inspiration and the area in which they wish to develop their creativity. Others will prefer more tangible media. If you are a tactile or kinesthetic person, you will not feel you are really creating anything unless you are fully physically involved. This could be by using the body in genres such as dance. Others might prefer a form more tangible and sensate: something that they can get their hands on and can get physically "stuck in to" to produce an expression of creativity that is real and has permanence. These become sculptors or potters.

Often people who are interested in creative forms that have a three-dimensional solidity to them have a spatial awareness more developed than most. Do you remember Steven Spielberg's film, *Close Encounters of the Third Kind*? Extraterrestrials try to make contact with humans through telepathy in order to bring them all to a particular spot, a strange-shaped mountain—the Devil's Tower National Monument in Wyoming. All over the world, a few individuals pick up the psychic signals and find different ways to express the image that starts to obsess them. Most doodle the distinctive shape of the mountain, but our hero, Roy Neary, played by Richard Dreyfuss, an ordinary blue-collar family man from Muncie, Indiana, is no artist; so he begins to sculpt the mountain—in mashed potato on his dinner plate.

RIGHT *Kinesthetic or tactile people might prefer the medium of dance.*

His bemused family sits around the table staring at him in alarm. Has he gone completely mad? Later he takes clay and begins to sculpt the mountain again, but still he isn't satisfied. He falls asleep by his creation then wakes up with a start. He thinks he has the answer! He knocks the top off the clay sculpture, leaving a flat-topped mountain. But still he is dissatisfied—it's not quite right. Finally, there is a wonderful scene where he tears up plants from his garden and throws barrow loads of earth through his window as he tries to make a model of what is in his head. He works all day in a frenzy until he has realized his vision—which is now a ceiling-high replica of Devil's Tower. When Neary and the others who have responded to the extraterrestrials' call arrive at Devil's Tower, the communication mode changes from image to sound. Through the universal language of music, species from different parts of the universe begin to communicate.

Roy Neary's chosen medium was three-dimensional, his dominant mode of creative expression, and he employed it instinctively and intuitively to represent the vision that was dominating his mind. Welcome then, to the wonderful world of clay! This is worth trying whether or not you are convinced that this is the way to your self-expression, whether you

would just like to check it out, or whether you just want to play.

ABOVE *In* Close Encounters of the Third Kind, *Roy Neary sculpts Devil's Tower.*

Experimenting with clay

Clay can be bought from most art supplies stores. If you are worried about the potential mess it might make, substitute children's modeling clay or other materials. Before trying to impose your will on the material—perhaps you have a clear idea of what you want to make from this substance—content yourself with just playing with it for a while. Knead it beneath your hands, squelch it around a bit, squeeze it, and shape it. In doing so, learn about its potential and possibilities. It is a solid material, yet wet and slippery, so it will lend itself to certain forms rather than others. It is given to solid, perhaps even bulky forms and shapes. Making long or towering skeletal figures like those of Swiss sculptor Alberto Giacometti, for example, is not going to work with this material, but bowls, heads, crouching figures of people, or animals—for these sorts of subjects clay is perfect. Take your clay and play. It can be a wonderful sensation as you knead and fashion the material into forms that represent what you want to portray. If you still have no clear idea of what it is that you want to make, try switching off the conscious brain. Let your hands and the clay come together. Let your hands be your brain and, in the synergy with the clay, see what is created. Once this has been done, then, and only then, can the conscious mind be brought into play. Now you can see what works and does not work so well. What line is good and what needs improvement? Refine it through this process and see what you develop. And the brilliant thing about clay is that, if you don't like what you produce, you can pummel it up back into a ball and try again. After all— tomorrow is another day.

ABOVE *Experience the potential of clay before trying to form shapes with it.*

Experimenting with plaster of Paris

Should you find that working with three-dimensional forms has a strong appeal, there are many other materials you can experiment with. Plaster of Paris is a great medium, although you have to work swiftly and intuitively as it sets fast. Once set, however, it is a perfect medium for carving. Before going into the detail of how to make statues and sculptures with plaster of Paris, try this simple way of making a bas-relief wall hanging. Take a square or round metal tray; some cookie sheets are good for this. The sheet's sides must be slanted outward and smooth so it acts as a mold. Grease it well, using light industrial oil, or cooking oil works just as well. Cut a loop out of a piece of leather and fasten it in one corner of the tray (if square) or somewhere on the edge if your tray is round. This will be the hanger for your finished piece of work. Then mix up the plaster and pour in to the tray. Allow it to set. Once it is hard—this should be a matter of minutes—turn the tray upside down and flex it. The plaster should pop out with the leather hanger firmly imbedded into it. You now have a shield or large medallion that can be hung up on the wall. The side that was against the tray is the side for you to work on. It should be beautifully smooth and white. Draw your design on to this side and then you can carve a bas-relief. Work out in advance what part of the design should be left in relief and what should be most recessed. With a sharp knife carve out the most recessed parts first and see the 3-D qualities of your design start to take shape before your eyes. The finished design can be left white, or painted and varnished, and then hung on your wall.

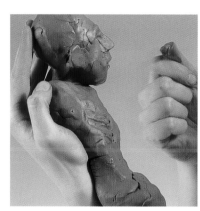

ABOVE *Switch off your mind and let your hands work with the clay.*

Sculpting

The beauty of this technique is that you can use the same mold time and again to make a series of wall carvings, or you can use different shapes and sizes of molds for different subjects and for different effects. Emboldened by this, why not try some free-standing sculpture?

For anything free standing that is taller than it is wide, you will need a framework—a skeleton to hold your structure together. For example, if you are making a sculpture from plaster you will find that while setting it will not stay, en masse, where you want it,

and once hard, it will be brittle and easy to break. You will need a skeleton to hold everything together. This does not have to be complicated. Find a strong but bendable piece of thick wire—old television aerials are brilliant for this—to form an armature. This will be the central support for your sculpture and other pieces of this material should be wired on firmly to indicate the general shape of your work. This should look like a "pin-man" version of the figure or form that you hope to create. This form should then be firmly nailed to a wooden base so that the whole of the structure is stable.

Now we have to bulk out our "pin man." Chicken wire is ideal. Chicken wire is a very thin, super-bendy wire mesh with about one-inch-wide gaps in the weave. It can be obtained from stores that sell garden and building products. The chicken wire can be crushed round the armature to form the approximate shape of your figure. Remember though to make it a smaller form than that of your finished figure, as plaster still has to be added on top. To keep the sculpture light but very strong, it is best not to try and infill this crush of wire with plaster. Instead, soak bandages or thin strips of cloth in a weak plaster solution and bind them tightly round your wire figure. Apart from making the structure much stronger, this will give you a clear idea of the finished form.

This is the Egyptian "mummy" stage. Is it how you envisioned it? More prosaically, are bits sticking out where they should not be? This is the time to make adjustments, because later you will not be able to carve through this base structure. Remember too, that this is a three-dimensional form. Walk round it, or twirl it around on a table. Does it work equally well from all angles. If

not, what should you change to make it work from every perspective? Sometimes it is useful to leave it for a while in another room. When you re-enter the room, it catches you off guard, as it were, and you see it with fresh eyes. You can see what works and what doesn't.

Once you are happy with this stage, mix up small amounts of plaster to add to your sculpture. It is better to mix small amounts at a time, so it does not set before you have time to apply it all. Focus on one bit at a time and then mix up more plaster to add to another bit. Slap it on and form the rough shapes you intend. Once the plaster is set, you can refine the detail by carving it with a sharp knife until it is beginning to look as you would

RIGHT *A vivid representation of the hands that create a sculpture.*

like it. You can continue this process of adding plaster and then carving it until you have it exactly right.

We have moved through a process of having an original idea to creating a "pin man." This developed through an Egyptian "mummy" stage to the finished work, which was achieved through a method of applying plaster and carving it away until the form was revealed. This makes the process sound very "you" driven; that you are in control and imposing your will and creative vision on the material. It can be like this, but you will often find that at some point—perhaps following the "mummy" stage and while applying the plaster on to the form—that the material takes control. It is assuming a form that is slightly different from your original vision. If this happens to you, go with it. You are not making an assembly line product here. This moment can signify the point when true creativity kicks in. It is when molder and molded, sculptor and sculpture become conjoined, become one. It is a special moment when the two "talk" to each other and work together to create something new and completely different, something truly original. It is the moment when a living creativity is born.

We have experimented with light and form. Let us now move on to playing with words.

remember

• No matter how mundane and familiar the scene, there are always different ways of looking at it to produce a new creative vision.

• "Observe, record, and interpret" is the way of the creative.

• Search for your lead means of creative expression. Do you think your creativity is best expressed through words and story-telling, pictures, music, dance, or sculpture?

• Experiment within your chosen modality: try out different styles, materials, forms, and genres.

• Fusing with your chosen medium to create something a little different from that which you planned is the spark that brings true creativity.

writing

Writing your creativity

" ...talents of the novelist:...observation of character, analysis of emotion, people's feelings, personal relations... "

VIRGINIA WOOLF, *novelist, writer of* A Room of One's Own

The most difficult part of writing is beginning. The second difficult thing is to keep going, and the third is knowing when to stop. The blank computer screen or blank page can be horrifyingly virgin territory. How do we mark it and will we merely spoil it? How to begin? Often the easiest way is not to start at the beginning. Just start anywhere. We also have to get used to the physical practice of writing. Like any skill, this is something that has to be acquired and then developed so we can then sit down and write with an easy familiarity. Ideally, you want to reach a state where this is as automatic as getting into your car and driving.

A way to begin is to get up in the morning, every morning and just write. Two or three pages each day

are plenty. This is not your novel, it is not your creative project; it is simply practicing the art of writing to attain an easy familiarity with the form. What you write about doesn't matter. Neatness, punctuation, and spelling do not matter. Just write. Let your hand transmit whatever is in your head at the time. Let it be a stream of consciousness. It could be a retelling of what went on the previous day; it could be describing a knotty problem that you have not found the answer to; it could relate to a fantasy. It could be about your children, your partner, your hopes and fears, what you intend to do today, your long-term goals, a thought-provoking television program from the night before. In short, it could be about absolutely anything. Just write. Don't even read it afterward. Put it safely away in a drawer. This practice might seem tedious and unnecessary, but it has been proven to work. It is almost as if the unblocking starts from the end of the process rather than at its beginning. Instead of consciously straining away to develop an idea or to find the right words to express your vision, there is almost a feedback from the hand to the brain that awakens the creative faculty. This process is called freewriting.

Freewriting

Freewriting was invented by Peter Elbow, professor of English at the University of Massachusetts, Amherst. Freewriting encourages you to do exactly what it says—to write freely,

ABOVE *The practice of freewriting is good for your creative expression.*

not worrying about what comes out of the end of your pen, its quality, or status. Your train of thought can do what thought often does naturally. It starts in one place and ends up somewhere completely different. You do not have to stick to the point, or stay "on message." You can write anything, on any subject. For the next 10 days, get up a bit earlier each morning and do 10 minutes of freewriting. This is good for your creative expression, even if your ambition is to be an artist or musician rather than a writer. There are some simple rules you should follow with freewriting (see page 85).

Creating not perfecting

In Albert Camus's famous novel *The Plague*, there is a character who introduces himself as a novelist, or at least as someone who is attempting to write one. Although the character has been working on his great work for several years, it has never progressed beyond the first line. This line, or at least the first version of it we read, is:

"One fine morning in the month of May an elegant young horsewoman might have been seen riding a handsome sorrel mare along the flowery avenues of the Bois de Boulogne."

This line is endlessly reworked as the character's intention is to produce the perfect sentence, the perfect opening line to what will inevitably be the perfect novel. At the end of Camus's book, this sad character is still no further forward; he is still working on that first line. Whatever you do, avoid this sterile fate. The first draft of your writing does not have to be perfect.

Finding ideas

"As you have seen, I am a writer who came of a sheltered life. A sheltered life can be a daring life as well. For all serious daring starts from within."

This is the first paragraph of the biography of writer Eudora Welty, who was born in the deep South and is now over 90 years old. Creativity can be born of trauma and struggle,

ABOVE *You don't have to have led a life of excitement to be full of creative inspiration.*

something to try

Freewriting

Unless you are an experienced creative writer, freewriting is best done with paper and pen, rather than a computer screen. Take some blank sheets of paper, your pen, and a clock or watch.

Decide that at a certain point you will start writing for 10 minutes and that after 10 minutes you will stop.

Don't worry about what to write about. You can write about anything— something that's happened to you recently, a fantasy, something you heard on the news, something one of your children said.

• Take any starting point and just write.

• Write quickly.

• Don't worry about spelling, punctuation, or how you are organizing the material. Let it flow.

If panic is setting in at this point, remember the famous maxim from Douglas Adams' novel *The Hitch-Hiker's Guide to the Galaxy*—DON'T PANIC. If you are sitting there paralyzed, not knowing what to write about, write about feeling paralyzed with fear. What do your muscles feel like in this state, what about your heart, your breathing? What position are your legs in? What sounds are you aware of in your environment? What does your fear taste like, smell like? What thoughts go through your mind in your state of panic? Now imagine another situation where you could be paralyzed with fear—experiencing some dramatic incident. Take what you know and project it into this new situation in order to imagine that situation. By now you will have enough material to write for hours.

but you don't have to have had severely traumatic or unusually exciting life experiences to be a creative person. Many woman writers, particularly from the 18th through to the early 20th century, when women's opportunities were more restricted, lived in the same area

with their families all their lives. No great world events impinged on them directly, but everything impinged on them indirectly and they found the material that fed their creativity in the daily drama of human life that surrounded them.

The English novelist Jane Austen lived a sheltered and protected life in rural southern England, making only occasional forays to London, the fashionable spa town of Bath, and to the sea. Not an amazing amount happened to her and her novels reflect this. Most deal with the issues faced by young upper-middle and upper-class women in finding a husband. Mistakes are made and painfully

ABOVE *The Aborigines have passed down stories from generation to generation.*

redeemed. Some fall in love with inappropriate people but, after learning from the heartbreak, they are saved by a "Mr. Right." There is not a lot of action if we are to compare her plots to typical Hollywood all-action blockbusters. Her novels are still read in the 21st century as avidly as when they were first written and they are frequently reworked into films. Director Ang Lee's version of *Sense and Sensibility* with Kate Winslett, Emma Thompson, Alan Rickman, and Hugh Grant is one of the many recent successes. Why should this be? Perhaps it is because she had acute observational skills and paid minute attention to the detail of those around her, whom she characterized vividly in her novels, bringing them fully to life on the page. Combined with her observational skills is an acute understanding of the manners and behavior of her day, leavened by a lucid style and a delightfully light ironic touch. No wonder her books still sell so well.

You don't have to have a lot happening in your life to become a successful writer. What you do need is acute observation, the ability to make your characters come alive, and a tale to tell that your readers can relate to.

I want to write: but how do I start?

What can you write about? If you are stuck for ideas, look at your own life. Most first novels are at least in part autobiographical. Many of the best first novels are written by people after the age of 40, so don't panic if you haven't started your great literary career and you are older than that. If you are older, you have more life experience, more knowledge, and more detachment and perspective. In other words, you have more resources to draw on. It makes sense to write about things that you do know in depth rather than things that

you don't, or only partly know. In order to create we need raw material to work with—words, symbols, visions, dreams, feelings, sensations, and experiences. This raw material comes from our imaginations and from our own experiences, and most often from the interaction between the two. To use the material that life has offered us creatively, we must learn to communicate it to others. One of the earliest forms of creative communication is story-telling. If you think that you are not a story-teller, you are wrong. We constantly tell narratives about ourselves. These narratives are masterpieces of story-telling. They are often stories in which we cast ourselves as hero or heroine in our struggle against the world. The version of our lives that we give to different people—friends, lovers, children, bosses—is not the same. We elaborate the story line, and create different narratives that select particular incidents as important and are designed to project carefully crafted versions of ourselves.

Mapping my life

Your life is a good source of ideas and a good starting point within your life experience is to create a lifeline. A lifeline is a way of mapping your life. To make your lifeline, you will need to draw, on separate pieces of paper, three graphs that look like this:

writing

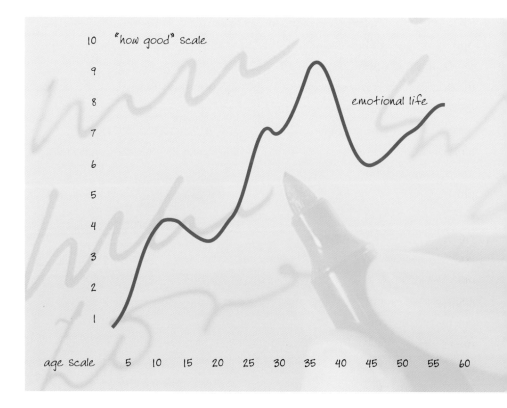

10   "how good" scale

9

8   emotional life

7

6

5

4

3

2

1

age scale   5   10   15   20   25   30   35   40   45   50   55   60

Use thin paper that you can see through or plastic laminate (the sort you get for overhead projectors) and make the scales on each graph identical. The scale at the bottom is for your age. Mark it off in yearly or five-yearly intervals. The left-hand scale marks how intense or good things were, how satisfied you felt with how you were doing. The higher the scale, the better you felt. You need three graphs because our lives are complex interwoven tapestries and we need to separate out some of the strands.

For the first graph, focus purely on the external aspects of your life—school, college, education, career, status in society, status with your peers, and so on. It is the external view of how you were doing at the ages on your graph. Mark off on the scale how good things were or how bad they were, how well things were going or how badly. Remember, the better things were the higher you mark your scale. When you went through bad or difficult times, mark it correspondingly lower. Make notes under the baseline to remind you what these highs and lows were. Then join up the marks and see what shape you get.

On the second sheet do exactly the same thing, but this time looking at your emotions and your emotional life, your feelings. Be honest with yourself. No one but you will see this.

Record how you felt through times of upheaval, through bereavements in the family, perhaps family splits. How did you feel when you first fell in love? When and how did it end, if it did? When did you feel most and least happy? Chart your emotional life. Do not try to justify how you felt, just plot the feeling.

For the third graph, try charting your self-fulfillment. This is a less tangible, more nebulous concept — but it can be done. Think about how good you felt about yourself at each of the stages in your life, how fulfilling your life was at each of these points, how much you were fulfilling your potential—the qualities and possibilities that are the inner you.

Now you have three graphs. Put the graphs on top of one other and hold them up to the light so you can see all three overlaying each other. Your graphs may look like jagged mountain peaks and deep valleys, or smooth and gentle ascents or descents, waves, or even swooping parabolas. What does this tell you about your life? Do the graphs follow roughly the same course or are there marked differences? Your external life might be smooth, but your emotional life almost frighteningly jagged. Are there significant points where all three graphs converge to a low that is very low, or a high that is almost off the scale? Are there points where the divergence is dramatic with one line going sharply one way while the other two go the other? Circle these significant points.

Significant points

These can be your starting points. They are times in your life when a lot was happening—either for good or bad. They are life-changing points from which we grow, sometimes immediately stronger, sometimes wounded but wiser, but from which we emerge with that wisdom painfully gained. Now select one of these points and begin to write about it. Should you choose a high point or a low point? Both are equally valid. It depends as to what strikes you as being the most compelling and what, to you, needs to be addressed the most urgently. Choosing a low point and writing your way through it can be a way of dealing with it in a more thorough manner than you may have been able to up to now. If you deal with it, you will feel such an upsurge in released energy that your creativity over the next few months might know no bounds. For every upside, however, there is always a downside. Some of these events might take so much working through that they deflect you away from the creative surge and leave you depressed for months. They have to be addressed at some point, but this may not be the right time.

It is easier and safer to choose an up point to start with. Look at it as an episode. What was it that came together to create such a high? Unravel the strands. Write about each strand as separate plot lines until finally they converge to create this ecstatic culmination. Suspend criticism and credulity while you write. Simply write and enjoy the experience. Don't worry about how much you write or how long it is. Just tell your story as simply and as naturally as possible. Let the word count take care of itself.

Once you have done this and you have produced something that expresses how you feel, leave it for quite a while. Go on to new things.

BELOW *Take a brave step out of the dark and into the light of creativity.*

66 *creativity is about talking to others, not about talking to yourself. Ask yourself, "Who is the audience?"* 99

DAVID BEATON,
theater director

Forget about it. Put it in a drawer. Return to it several months later. Now, coming to it fresh, how does it read? This is time for your appraisal faculties to come into play—but not too much. Do not let the "judgmental adult" come storming in, swamping your entire creative endeavor in negative criticism. Read it with the freshness of new eyes. Does it read well? Can you follow the story line? Does it engage your emotions? Do you gain from reading it? Hopefully you will answer yes to most of these questions. Yes, you will probably see areas where things could have been said better. There might even be bits that make you wince. Is that, however, a "good" wince—reflecting things so sharply they still cause a reaction in you—or a "bad" wince— you were over the top on that; you wish you had expressed things differently? You decide.

Whatever the case, you now have a story line, a narrative, which sees things from a single perspective—your own. This can be developed further. Who are the other characters in the story? How do they come across? Are they just foils or passive participants, are they real characters or are they two dimensional, perhaps even one dimensional, in comparison with the strong "I"-driven narrative? What would happen if you rewrote the story from one of these characters' perspectives? It is an enriching and rewarding experience. Try it.

Empathizing

When you begin to explore the perspective of the other players in your private drama, you are beginning to empathize with other people's viewpoints. When we read a great story or see a painting that inspires us, when we hear a poem that moves us, or a piece of music that fills us with joy, it is because the artist who created it has succeeded in conveying to us some of his or her own experience. That is not all. We must not only translate our ideas and visions into form, we must do so in a way that others can understand. Our experiences can be deeply meaningful to us, but meaningless to others. They become art when they communicate something that is common to all of us, a shared human experience. When we read a good story, it may grip us because it is intense or exciting, but it

will also grip us because we recognize in it an expression of true human emotion, thought, and experience. We recognize ourselves in the story and those around us. In other words, the story transcends the personal to become transpersonal, the shared experience of us all.

The first stage of creativity is to create something that speaks to us, that expresses our own experience. This may or may not achieve "creative transcendence," when we create something that speaks powerfully to others. Many of our adolescent writings, and particularly teenage poetry, are deeply meaningful to us at the time, but embarrassing in their self-focus when we read them years later. They were intensely important to our personal emotional expression, but not to someone else. What all truly creative people have in

66 The whole difference between construction and creation is exactly this: that a thing constructed can only be loved after it is constructed; but a thing created is loved before it exists. 99

MARGARET ATWOOD, *novelist*

writing

something to try

Finding another voice

Everything that happens to us is material that we can use for our creative expression. We know more about ourselves than anything else in our world, so "me" is a good place to start, but in order to become a writer, you need to take other voices, to become "not me" or "another me." This is an exercise to imagine someone else's life. Choose one of these characters, one that is definitely not you, and write about starting school.

• You are a middle-class African American child living in a predominantly white neighborhood. Your mother is a doctor and your father manages a local supermarket.

• You are Irish and your parents come from Dublin, but they came to London to work in the IT industry and you were born in England. They have just moved back to Dublin and you are starting school for the first time. You have an English accent.

• You live in a small Bible-belt town in Kentucky. Your mom left home when you were two years old. Your father, a preacher, has brought you up.

• You live in a small rural community. Your parents are farmers, as were their parents and grandparents before them. Times are hard and everyone in the area is poor.

• You are British. You have been living with your father and mother in Saudi Arabia, where your father works for an oil corporation. You are the oldest child and are being sent back to England to go to boarding school. It is the school that your father attended and his father before him.

• Your mother is very young. She became pregnant in her midteens. Her boyfriend deserted her and her parents kicked her out. She works in a fast food store to support you both and you are used to spending long hours at a nursery. You know she loves you, but when you are together she is always completely exhausted.

common is the ability to express human emotion. Many of our greatest musicians and artists had emotional lives that were lived in great turmoil just because they felt so intensely.

Passion

Theater director David Beaton says, "Creativity is about loving what you are creating." Creativity cannot exist without passion—hence the hopeless love lives of many of the world's great writers, composers, and painters. We must feel. We must know what intense emotion is. Passion begets passion. If a work does not engage us emotionally, it may be able to teach us facts, but it is not a creative work, a work that inspires human emotion, inspiration, and passion. Even abstract painting often communicates symbolic representations of states of feeling.

Intense emotion can be channeled into creative endeavor, bringing release. To be creative, we have to be prepared to become involved in life and living. We need to be aware of the dilemmas of individual lives and of the history of our species and of the crises that face us now. We also need to understand the emotions of others. Emotions are to writers what colors are to painters. Writers need to have an abundant emotional vocabulary—a range of ways of expressing feelings and "feeling into" the minds, hearts, and experiences of others. This requires empathizing, something that people with a strong feeling function can do more readily than those of us who are intellectual thinkers. Thinkers can write great novels, but unless they can flesh out their characters' emotions, their novels will not engage the wider

66 A ratio of failures is built into the process of writing. The wastebasket has evolved for a reason. 99

MARGARET ATWOOD,
novelist

ABOVE *Never give up on your attempts to express your creativity.*

ABOVE *Much data for our creative work can be gathered at pavement cafés.*

Becoming a people-watcher

A writer is a people-watcher and a people-listener. Have you ever wondered why creative Americans and Europeans were drawn to Paris in the 19th century? One of the reasons was the European café society that developed into a fine art in Paris. Paris today is still full of pavement cafés where artists and intellectuals gather to sit outside, watching the passers-by and listening avidly to conversations at neighboring tables. We mix with others and hear snatches of conversation, episodes from other lives. We are gathering data to feed our creative imaginations.

If you are an extrovert, you may find it easier to write while you are surrounded by other people chatting and laughing. As a student, I (Vivianne) wrote half of the essays for my first degree in a café next door to a drama college. The colorful drama students who came in during their breaks were stimulating enough to see me through the most boring psychology essay. I wrote the other half of my essays in the quieter environment of the university library surrounded by other students beside a picture window that opened out on to parkland. I learned a lot about the social and sex life of squirrels—and wrote some excellent essays.

public. They will appeal only to other intellectuals like themselves—and since many intellectuals read non-fiction rather than novels this is a small market. Empathy means understanding how your characters might feel. This is not the same as understanding how you might feel in a particular situation.

Much of our early fiction writing will be about representing the voices of our sub-personalities—the different aspects of our own selves that we sometimes keep hidden. We are literally engaging in a dialog with ourselves—and it is unlikely to be of interest to anyone else. As our writing moves forward and as we mature in our understanding of other people around us, we will be able to more truly express the experiences, feelings, and world view of people who are very different from ourselves.

The Restaurant Game

This is all about creating stories about your fellow diners. It is very simple. For developing plot lines, character, and one's own imagination, busy restaurants are hard to beat. This game also works best if you are with someone who will play it with you, as your imaginations and inspirations can spark off each other.

All you have to do is be observant. Watch a neighboring table. Who is there? What might have brought them together? Gauge this from how they talk to each other, their body language, their relationship in terms of age, how they dress, their moods, and whether their moods are coinciding or opposed. Imagine a scenario that might have got them together at this particular table. How have they come together? What is the nature of the relationship? Is it cordial or hostile? Is one on the make? Is this a new or existing relationship? Is it going through good or bad times? Imagine what they might be saying and project forward; how might this story end? Based on this acute observation of this "Brief Encounter" you might develop a complete short story. There are just two things to remember: you are not interested in the real facts or what the truth might be. Secondly, don't choose a table that is too close to your own!

We have played with our creativity and are beginning to befriend it. Do we now want to make a deeper commitment to our creativity?

remember

- Just practice writing: you are not attempting the perfect, finished novel.

- You have more ideas in your head than you could ever write about: all you have to do is access them.

- Your life so far holds many stories: there are untold riches here.

- There is a story behind everything you encounter, behind your friends and contacts and behind every scene that you see.

- Open up your imagination to the possibilities of what is around you and all will be shown to you.

committing

Committing to your creativity

"Until one is committed, there is always a hesitancy,

the chance to draw back, always ineffectiveness.

Concerning all acts of initiative (and creation),

there is one elementary truth, the ignorance of which

kills countless ideas and splendid plans:

that the moment one definitely commits oneself,

then Providence moves too.

All sorts of things occur to help one

that would never otherwise have occurred.

A whole stream of events issue from the decision,

raising in one's favor all manner of unforeseen incidents

and meetings and material assistance, which no man

could have dreamed would have come his way. I have

learned a deep respect for one of Goethe's couplets:

'Whatever you can do, or dream you can, begin it:

boldness has genius, power, and magic in it; begin it

now.'"

W.H. MURRAY,
leader of the Scottish Himalayan Expedition

We cannot realize our creative potential until we are willing to commit ourselves to expressing our creativity. "Commitment" is a word that suggests hard work. Work is part of the creative process, of course, but we have also talked about unleashing our creative energies through play, through having fun. It can be fun to discover your potential and abilities, through what you create. The most successful creative people are those who can combine a sense of fun and wonder with serious application. Nobody can pick up a pen, a musical instrument, some clay, a box of pastels, or a paintbrush and immediately become a maestro. It is dedicated practice that buttresses the creative surge. Practice that is fun produces focused play.

> 66 I cannot help considering it a sign of talent that I do not give it up, though I can get nobody to take an interest in my efforts. 99

FANNY MENDELSSOHN, *pianist and composer, sister of Felix Mendelssohn, composer*

Persevering

No one achieved anything without hours of practice and the more ideas you have, the more likely you are to hit the "big one." It is important, though, not to have unrealistic expectations about the time it takes to

BELOW *Like a mountaineer, we must take bold steps toward the summit.*

ABOVE *All artists must practice and persevere with their craft to improve.*

become good at what we do. Research shows that great artists, writers, and scientists take 10 years from when their first work appears to when they begin to show mastery in their chosen profession. This is 10 years of patient hard work. To be creative we need time that we set aside for creative work. Once you have taken these first steps to exercise your creativity through exercising your imagination—and the imagination is like a muscle in the mind, it needs to work and the more it works, the stronger it gets—it is good to make your creative intent public. Just like when we resolve to give up smoking or drinking, we

know we are not truly for real if we keep quiet about it. Doing it privately is implicitly embracing failure. If it doesn't work, nobody will know; nobody can criticize if you fail. By making our commitment to creativity public, we are not talking about a grand announcement; just tell selected people. When you meet these people and they inquire after you, tell them what you are "becoming."

"I am working to become a writer/painter/violinist or whatever." This reinforces your intention, encouraging you to stick with it and to become what you are setting out to be—a creative person.

Improving

Creativity is fun, joyous, inspiring, enlivening—and hard work. There is always that point when it is easier to give up than go on. Creativity feeds on forward movement. It is important not to stand still. When you have achieved a creative work that satisfies you—whether it is an artwork, literary work, work project, or piece of craftwork, then ask yourself—what next? What can I do that will consolidate the skills that I have used, but that at the same time will push the boundaries of what I think I can do? To express our creativity, we must be emotionally resilient. It is rare for anyone's first creative efforts to be fully appreciated. To get recognition, we must keep plugging away at our chosen medium, improving the quality of our work with each attempt, until we make that breakthrough, when people suddenly see our work as though for the first time and think—this is good!

Our creativity must have channels to flow through so we need to perfect our technique. Musicians must play, singers must sing, dancers must dance, painters must paint, and writers must write in order to experiment with their medium and to try out new avenues. Once you have experimented and found your medium, you start to grow in confidence. Now is the stage to learn from other creative people working in the same medium. If you want to be a painter, learn everything you can about different techniques, try different materials, go to classes,

workshops, and study groups to experiment with others, visit artists in their studios, and exhibitions of artists' work. Remember, you are not looking for ideas and creative inspiration, you are looking for hand skills. If you want to write, read other people's work, but you are not reading to engage with their stories. You are reading to discuss what works and why. Ask yourself questions as you are reading: does the characterization work—or are these people cardboard cut-outs? What are the twists and turns of the plot? Does it unfold too easily—can you predict the ending when you are just 10 pages into chapter one? In a nonfiction work, ask yourself does it engage the reader—and how? Is the writing lively and clear? Does the writer use imagery, analogy, and examples to give life to the text? Read newspaper columns and feature writers and see how they use their restricted space and how much they can convey in only a few thousand words. Remember, when you look at other people's work, you are not seeking to copy what they do. You are examining the range of possibilities and seeking to discover your own style.

Learning from others

Creativity requires time spent on our own, but we also need to meet other creative people who can inspire and

> 66 An artist does not skip steps; if he does, it is a waste of time because he has to climb them. 99
>
> JEAN COCTEAU, *filmmaker*

stimulate us, and give us the support we need. There are many different ways of meeting others. You can meet people through classes where there is someone to teach and guide you, or you can meet other people in writers', artists', or other creative peer groups.

Attending classes that help you to perfect your techniques in your chosen medium can be enormously helpful in launching you on your creative path. However, a poorly run class and a bad teacher can put you off for life. If you live in a small town, you may not have much option about where you go to learn, but often you will have choices ranging from university or college courses to private courses or lessons given by individual artists, writers, or other creative workers. The best way of finding a good course is by word of mouth. Ask around. Ask friends, neighbors, your children's teachers. A good class is one where people enjoy themselves. Attending courses is hard work and if you don't enjoy yourself when you get

66 It is the supreme art of the teacher to awaken joy in creative expression and knowledge. 99

ALBERT EINSTEIN,
quantum physicist

there, you will think of a thousand reasons not to go. People usually enjoy themselves when there is a stimulating environment that encourages them to learn and work. We all need constructive criticism, but an overly critical teacher may crush our confidence at the beginning so we give up. Early on, we need constant encouragement, rather than criticism. Think of creativity as a small child that you are raising. Your creative self needs to be able to discern good and bad work, but more importantly it needs lots of encouragement to persist when it hits a creative block or when something just won't go right.

Remember that a good artist or writer is not necessarily a good teacher. In fact, many of the qualities that distinguished some highly creative people—such as the ability to work alone for long periods—are not the qualities that make for good teaching. Good teachers want to engage with others and get as much pleasure from others' success as from their own. In addition, a personal chemistry exists with a good teacher. My (Vivianne's) favorite math teacher was an elderly, retired, long-sighted gentleman who enlivened each lesson by falling off the platform around his desk as he walked further and further back, trying to see what he had written on the board. On first appearance, he seemed like an eccentric otherworldly professor, totally out of contact with everyday reality. This impression was largely correct, but he was in contact with reality in that he was brilliant at explaining mathematical concepts. He used everything from plain logical language to poetic metaphor. After a few months of his teaching, I decided that I just loved algebra. It became a logical problem-solving game, and the sheer enjoyment of solving the puzzle was intense. He was a highly creative person in that he could create in us, his adolescent pupils, enthusiasm, joy, understanding, and even some passion—for math!

Creative peers

When you start your creative work, meeting with others who are walking a creative path is a source of stimulation and support. When you begin to commit yourself to creativity, you may have to go out consciously to find such people. Once you begin your creative work, you will find that it acts like a beacon and draws other creative people to you. However small your local town or city, you will find there are other creative people

there. There may be art groups, writing groups, readers' circles who meet to discuss new books, photography clubs, theater groups—the list is endless. As well as activities in your own area, look for weekend workshops and classes and summer residential weeks. Partners and children can often come on writing and painting holidays too. As these are often held in beautiful, foreign surroundings, this is no hardship. By meeting with others for discussions, classes, or simply to socialize, you will be stimulated by

ABOVE *Painting holidays allow you to meet with other artists.*

their ideas and enthusiasm, learn about new techniques, pick up on the latest trends, and share the miseries of writer's block. You can give and get emotional support when the long-protracted negotiation ends only in a rejection slip, and with the other vagaries of the creative life that occur. Sharing the triumphs of others and consoling them for their disappointments will help you realize that you are not alone; that others are struggling along with you and that the difficulties you encounter day-to-day are normal and par for the course if you want to win through to success.

Creating time

To improve our technique we must practice. Practice requires time. For most of us, time is a precious and scarce commodity. Whether we are jobholders, parents, or students, and maybe even all three, it can be a struggle to fit in all our existing commitments. How on earth are we to create, carve out, free up, an extra chunk of this rare commodity, time, in order to do something that might seem, at least to a part of our brain, a self-indulgence, a frippery, a distraction from the important business of life? There is no straightforward answer. One person's solution won't work for everyone. Many find that they are most creative at the beginning of the day. Others are night owls who work better when the streets grow quieter and the rest of the household is asleep. We can produce more creatively if we learn to work with our brain and body rhythms than if we try to force them into artificial patterns that are not in harmony with them. Creating is a bit like dieting. A regular rhythm that does not strain the body works better than intensive focusing on the activity, which exhausts us, and leads us to lapse back into our old ways. Some will want to work at their project everyday; others find, either by circumstances or through preference, that this is too much, and that an hour or two a week, perhaps over the weekends, suits them best. You have to find your own rhythm but once found, do stick to it.

Establishing a creative rhythm is important. There is an old saying in experimental psychology that "spaced practice is better than massed practice." If we work at something in regular bursts, we do not stop "working" on it when we down tools. Our minds are still processing information and integrating ideas and inspirations. If you write or paint, you are likely to find that when you wake up in the morning your ideas have moved forward during the night. The tricky bit of the plot that was holding you up yesterday seems to have a solution today. We learn better if we practice something for a while, then leave it for a while, and then practice it again. We can pass a driving test

66 When you are completely absorbed or caught up in something, you become oblivious to things around you, or to the passage of time. It is this absorption in what you are doing that frees your unconscious and releases your creative imagination. 99

ROLLO MAY,
psychotherapist

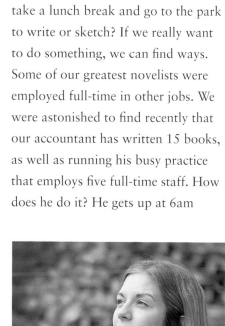

more easily if we practice for an hour a day over a period of a few weeks than if we go on an intensive course where we have to practice for hour after hour. This is because in between the practice sessions, our brains process the information they have learned. They integrate the techniques into automatic sequences that flow one from another. If we do not have this "processing time" we cannot integrate new skills and information so quickly. Creative thought and creative expression work similarly to learning. If we work for a while and take regular breaks, then we produce better quality work.

We may not have the luxury of large blocks of time that we can devote to our creative work. It may be an hour before the children wake up, in the afternoon before collecting them from school, late at night when your partner is getting ready for bed, or mid-evening when he or she is slumped in front of the television. For many people, the idea of finding a whole hour every day for their creative projects might seem impossible, but try thinking about exactly how you spend every hour of your day. Could you get up earlier, go to bed later, not watch television in the evening, or

take a lunch break and go to the park to write or sketch? If we really want to do something, we can find ways. Some of our greatest novelists were employed full-time in other jobs. We were astonished to find recently that our accountant has written 15 books, as well as running his busy practice that employs five full-time staff. How does he do it? He gets up at 6am

chapter 7

RIGHT *A lunch break provides a window of time in which to write or draw.*

every morning and writes for one hour a day before having breakfast, driving the children to school, and then going on to work. The 500 words a day that he has trained himself to write every Monday to Friday have built into 15 published books. Similarly, many of our most famous composers worked long years as music teachers and many artists have had to fund their artwork by all manner of part-time jobs. To get somewhere you have to find your hour.

Whether the one-hour-a-day method will work for you will depend on your creative medium. If you want to make pottery, or work with another process that requires the preparation of complex materials, then it won't; but for drawing, painting, writing, and many craft skills, it will. Once you know that you only have to find, initially at least, one hour a day, then the creative task becomes easier. You are not asking the impossible of yourself. You are not demanding drastic changes in your lifestyle and, just as importantly, you can develop a

ABOVE *Take regular exercise breaks to free your mind.*

positive psychological attitude to the fact that your creative activity can only take up an hour of your day. We can think of the other activities that we must do as helpful breathing space, rather than irritating distractions. This is important psychologically. We can think of our creative work as an ongoing process with breaks for other things, but in our unconscious minds, the creative process is continuing. Even if we can only work for one hour a day, psychologically this can be a primary commitment. Other important activities in our lives—a paid job, parenting, caring for our partner, an educational course—are all life material and experience that we can draw on to enhance our creative imagination. Everything that we do, see, hear, feel, and think during the course of the day is food for our creative brains.

If we have periods when we can work uninterrupted, it is still important to take regular breaks. Spend 5 minutes each hour just walking around or doing some stretching exercises. When our muscles become tense, this restricts our energy flow and restricts our creative thought process. Five minutes of yoga an hour is an excellent way of stimulating ourselves creatively. Every two hours, we need to take a slightly longer break of 10-15 minutes to take a drink and walk around. If we can go outside, so much the better.

Remember that in Christian contemplative monastic orders, much of their praying and meditation was done while walking around their cloisters. We can use these breaks to think—where next? What is the next stage in the process that I need to tackle? As well as walking, more vigorous exercise is a good way of "breaking set," of allowing the conscious mind to let go of the creative process and the unconscious to take over. Jogging, walking, dancing, and swimming are all good rhythmic activities that allow our bodies to be released from tensions, increase oxygen to the brain, and release endorphins that give us physical highs.

Creating space

To be creative we need to allocate ourselves some space. Early 20th-century novelist Virginia Woolf wrote a book called *A Room of One's Own*. Not all of us can aspire to have our own room. However, we can aspire to have a table, desk, portfolio, creative journal, or computer that is ours and is not for sharing. For mothers especially, it can be hard to set aside space that is "mine alone" and is not for a partner's clutter or children's sticky fingers, but to own our creativity we must stake a claim to some small private space.

A creative person needs a setting in which to express his or her creativity. We also need a setting that is a manifestation of our creative expression. We can express our creativity through everything around us—our homes, work environment, clothes, hair, and personal style.

Equally important is creating your environment as an aspect of your creative self. This is your own creative space where you will be giving your creativity a chance to flower and to

66 Creativity is the result of your personal growth, self-awareness, and strength of style—an expression of your personal philosophy of life. It is the way that you try to make an impression on someone else, your whole aura—the way you speak, dress, walk. We create an image of ourselves and how we want to project it. 99

KEVIN HOPKINS,
hair stylist

> 66 If you want a golden rule that will fit everything, this is it: have nothing in your houses that you do not know to be useful, or believe to be beautiful. 99

WILLIAM MORRIS,
craftsman

grow. You could imagine it as an incubation chamber for your creativity. What do you need around you to foster your creative vision?

Both of the points made by William Morris in the quotation above are equally important. Your space has to be functional; it has to work for you. Yet, shouldn't it also inspire? If possible, paint the walls of the room in which you do your creative work in colors that will influence your mood. Bright primary colors—especially red—convey energy and dynamism. More muted pastel tones—especially blues and violets—make for a soothing, reflective environment. Surround yourself with beautiful items, both natural and manmade, and with symbols that are relevant to you. If you are using your hands, whether in writing or any of the visual arts, you might like to play music for some of the time when you are working. An

artist friend of ours got over all manner of creative blocks by playing classical symphonies. She then painted what she heard. This developed to a sequence of paintings that she successfully exhibited. Creativity feeds from the creativity of others. Similarly, share your creative space with a living plant so that your creativity and the plant can grow together.

Being prepared for your creativity

If you want to commit yourself to expressing your creativity, you need to set aside time when your creative projects can be given your full attention. Creativity isn't, however, a tap that you can turn on and off at will. Once you are in touch with your creative spirit, you will need to be able to respond to the moment. Ideas can come at any time; not just when we decide that this is the day we are going to work on our project. Get used to taking something with you to record your ideas. Writers always carry a notebook. Get a nicely bound book that you enjoy writing in and that is esthetically pleasing. Some of my (Vivianne's) best ideas come from listening to conference papers— boring conference papers. My mind switches off and needs something to occupy it. Ideas begin to well to the surface. Usually something in the paper has created an association and that creates another association. A chain begins to form and soon we are far away from our apparent starting point. I devised the synopsis for a book I wrote on Kabbala from listening to a lecture about the psychologist Carl Jung's trip to India in the 1930s. In fact, this was a very interesting conference paper, but it was a subject I already knew. In no time, my mind had switched from thinking about Indian deities to

BELOW *A pleasant, private working space will enhance your creativity and allow ideas and sensations to flow unchecked.*

committing

chapter 7

committing

ABOVE *The sculptor Barbara Hepworth's garden in St. Ives, Cornwall, England—an outpouring of her great talent.*

thinking about deity in other traditions and the next thing I knew I was writing a book synopsis on the back of the conference timetable. Nowadays, I would have my lovely purple spiral-bound notebook and there would be a lot less risk of my losing my precious synopsis. You may find that ideas come to you just before you go to sleep or when you wake up. It may be in a restaurant, on the way home from visiting a friend, or waiting in the airport for a delayed flight. Wherever you are, be ready to write down your ideas. If you are a photographer, pictures can turn up at any time. As well as any more sophisticated camera you own, keep a small camera that you can carry with you. If you paint or draw, you will need a small sketchpad. Ideas, links, witty phrases, visual images—your life is surrounded by potential material. Once you are alert to it, you will notice it all the time, so be ready to record it wherever you are.

We have played, explored, learned, and committed. Now we must go a stage further with our personal creative process. We must go to the place of the Holy Mystery, the place of transformation.

remember

• Yes, getting somewhere creatively will involve practicing and lots of hard work: it can also be fun.

• Ignore the siren voices of the critics and the negative doubt in your head. Listening to critics while creating only leads to a compromise. Compromises don't work.

• Creativity feeds creativity. Surround yourself with creative things and stimulating creative people.

• Spaced practice is better than massed practice—we need breaks from the creative effort to allow the conscious mind to let go and the unconscious to get to work.

• Once started, the creative flow is like a geyser or hot water spring; it can erupt suddenly. Be prepared and always have the necessary materials at hand to record your creative ideas.

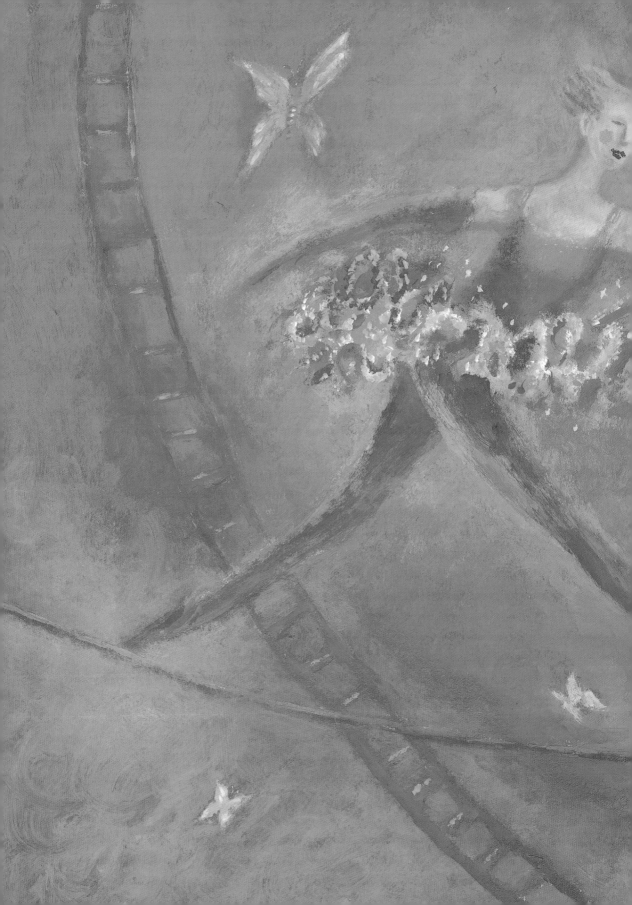

chapter 8

transforming

Transforming your creativity

"*Far away there in the sunshine are my highest aspirations. I may not reach them, but I can look up and see their beauty, believe in them, and try to follow where they lead.*" LOUISA MAY ALCOTT, *novelist*

Creativity is an alchemical process. We bring together memories, dreams, sensory impressions, and skills. A synthesis occurs that produces a result—our personal alchemical gold—that is greater than the sum of the parts. Psychologists who have studied creativity and creative people agree that the creative process has four stages: preparation, incubation, illumination, and verification. If we understand these four stages, we can begin to understand our creative processes better. These four stages can be equated with the four elements of alchemy—earth, water, fire, and air.

ABOVE *Like all meditative practices, yoga helps us sustain concentration.*

Preparing—Earth

The element of earth relates to practical preparations. We think about what we want to do and begin to work on the task. Perhaps we decide we want to paint a picture. We assemble the materials we might need and assess the advantages of different types of paint. We might do some preliminary sketches. Our conscious mind is working on the project using the knowledge and skills that we already possess.

At this stage, we might have a new creative insight that is going to be the basis of our new work—or we may not. We may have decided to write a novel. We may have an idea of the genre of novel we want to write. We may have looked at other books of that type. Perhaps we have a preliminary story line. Often this will be derivative—almost a synthesis of other work we have read. There is nothing wrong with derivative work—it can be highly successful, but it does not yet have something unique about it, something that comes from deep inside us and marks it as truly "ours." We are creating using left-brain activity, conscious thought based on our existing skills and knowledge.

We can help prepare our brains for creativity by teaching them certain skills. In order to do our creative work, we need to be able to focus our attention. Having something to work on that we enjoy will help us focus our attention anyway, but we can enhance our ability to concentrate by taking up meditation, yoga, t'ai chi, martial arts, or similar practices. From meditation to martial arts might seem a sudden swing from passive stillness to aggressive violence, but in reality both extremes of Eastern practise concentrate on building up certain mental skills—the ability to focus, to hold a certain amount of information in our field of concentration at once, and the ability to cut out extraneous distractions. There is a close relationship between physiological arousal and our concentrative abilities. The more physiologically aroused we are, the more our attention will switch from one thing to another. Meditative practices of all kinds reduce physiological arousal, help us relax, and enable us to have sustained concentration.

Incubating–Water

Water is the incubation stage of creativity when we may step back from our project. We "let go." We stop worrying and consciously thinking about it. People often speak of the "three Bs" of creativity—bed, bath, and the bus. When we are not consciously pursuing the problem, a new answer comes in an unexpected

RIGHT *Always follow where your aspirations are leading you.*

Incubating—Water

In the silence that rings with sound,

I am still and hear your voice.

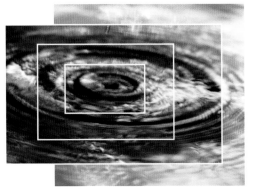

The transition of the formless

into words—

the mind a still, receptive pool.

A thought drops in, disappearing—

a stone without splashing,

and rests in the depths,

the waters digesting it—slowly.

Is the stone a pearl?

VIVIANNE CROWLEY

way. This can happen with everything from a crossword puzzle clue to remembering where we put something that we've lost, to finding the solution to a scientific problem, or the next scene in a screenplay—the stage is set for new insights to emerge. The elements of the problem are seen in a new way that allows a solution. This doesn't mean of course that we have stopped thinking about our creative project. This stage may last only a few minutes. We let go and suddenly we have a new insight that lifts our ideas on to a more creative level. The incubation period can also last days, weeks—even years. When we let go, the preoccupations, preconceptions, and existing habits of thought that we have used so far are released. We can actively encourage this relaxation process and the switch to a different type of thinking through techniques used by creative human beings for millennia. When seeking a creative vision in order to write a poem or solve a problem, people as diverse as Inuit shamans and Irish druids used the same method. They would go to a secluded hut, block up the windows, lie down, have an assistant place heavy stones on their stomachs to hold them down, and then be left in the darkness for ideas and visions to come. Today, the flotation tank is the slightly more comfortable equivalent. In a flotation tank, we are left to float in the darkness on warm, salty, and therefore buoyant water. Soft music can be played and our brains in this womblike atmosphere will begin to process new material. If you do not live near a large city that possesses a flotation tank, but you do have a bath, then you can create your own relaxation session at home. Make sure you have plenty of hot water. Fill a bath, adding some perfumed bath oil or foam, light the room with perfumed candles, switch off the electric light, and relax in your bath.

Scientists believe that in conditions of darkness and lack of disturbing or intrusive sounds, our left brain ceases to be so dominant and the right brain takes over. The right brain processes spatial information and sees wholes and symbols. Our brain patterns also change. In our normal waking state, our brains work at a high frequency called beta rhythm. In states of complete relaxation and slight sensory deprivation, our brains produce two lower frequencies—alpha rhythm, which is associated with relaxation, and theta rhythm, which is associated with dreaming and producing images. Another way of taking our brains into these states while still awake is through meditation. If you find that you cannot settle down to creative work because your mind is over-busy and cannot focus on what you are doing, take a few classes in a meditative practise that you can use just before you start your creative sessions. This will help clear your mind of all the trivia that can distract you so that you can focus on your creative process. Yoga is another useful technique, and it has the advantage of helping our bodies become more physically harmonious.

Illuminating-Fire

Incubation leads to illumination. In the illumination stage of the creative process, new ideas arrive in our mind with a suddenness that can be like a fiery lightning flash. As well as the relaxation states that we have described under the incubation section, our brains process ideas while we are asleep. This is the time when the conscious mind can communicate with the unconscious. In space and silence, the voice of the creative unconscious can be heard. When we

66 When I am... completely myself, entirely alone... or during the night when I cannot sleep, it is on such occasions that my ideas flow best and most abundantly. Whence and how these come I know not nor can I force them... nor do I hear in my imagination the parts successively, but I hear them together all at the same time. 99

WOLFGANG AMADEUS MOZART, *composer*

difficult to believe, but it is important to remember that nearly all creative writers do their writing in the morning. The typical pattern for a creative writer is to write when his or her conscious mind is as near the unconscious world of dream, vision, and sleep as possible. This is when we first get up in the morning. If you force yourself to write early in the morning you will find that however difficult it seems to begin, if you persist, ideas will pour out of you.

sleep, the conscious mind sleeps, but the brain does not sleep. It continues to process the events, impressions, intuitions, stimulations, frustrations, joys, hopes, and fears of the day, even though we are not aware of it. It categorizes them, attempts to classify them and to integrate them with past experiences, to create links with what has gone before. Many of you will know that you wake up full of ideas. Others, who find that dragging themselves out of sleep is like the journey of humankind's evolution from the primeval slime, will find this

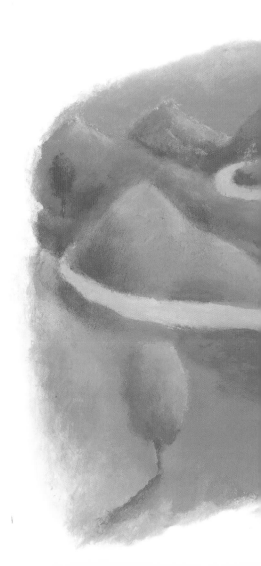

RIGHT *Stick to your chosen creative path and follow it to its natural end.*

You may find that once you have started a creative project, you wake up in the morning with ideas for whole new images if you are producing art work, or aspects of characterization or plot if you are writing fiction. Projects that reach a blockage often miraculously move forward once the right hemisphere of the brain, which thinks more holistically than the left hemisphere, can get to work on them. The right brain's overview takes the project on to a different level and we begin to move forward again. We can tell that the right brain has become active if we find that we get new insights via strong visual images. Visual images are not only important in artistic creativity. They can also provide valuable new insight into scientific investigations.

The images that emerge during the illumination phase of creativity often appear to come very quickly. They are "bolts from the blue," "inspirations," the "aha effect." This sudden and apparently random factor makes the creative process seem illogical and mysterious. Sigmund Freud, founder of psychoanalysis, was happy to think that everything could be explained through his psychoanalytic theories—except for creativity. Since creative ideas often seem to appear "out of the blue," all cultures associate creativity with Divine inspiration. Religions with multiple gods, such as Hinduism, have some who are especially associated with creativity. In Irish tradition, creativity is one of the gifts of the goddess Brigid, who became St. Bridget when Ireland became Christian. Creativity is also a gift of the many-talented god Lugh, a harper, poet, silversmith, and much else besides. Lugh is associated in Celtic myth with sunlight and Brigid with fire. Light and fire give illumination in the darkness so are natural symbolic images that often appear in connection

with creativity. A simple way of speaking to our unconscious minds to remind them that they are about to assist us with creative work is to light a perfumed candle just before we start. As you do so, you can say something to remind yourself that creative inspiration comes from a deeper source of your being than your everyday conscious mind. It comes from a deeper level that is present within all of us. We have only to access it.

Verifying—Air

Verification is the final stage of the creative process. This involves our left brains and our logical rational judgment, which equates with the element of air.

Once we have had the creative illumination, we need to turn this into a piece of creative work. To do this, we must once again draw on what we know. We must use our knowledge, our skills, memories of previous work, to test out the idea. Does the seemingly perfect plot for a novel that popped up from our unconscious minds seem practical in the light of day? Look at it carefully. Our logical linear left brain comes into play once more to test out the new idea and whether it can work.

ABOVE *Stimulate your senses to enrich the raw material.*

Transforming— The Creative Spirit

The final element of the creative journey is spirit, that mysterious fifth element that is both within and beyond the other four. When our creative work achieves transcendence, when it speaks to others in deep and powerful ways, then we touch on the realm of the spirit. This book is part of a journey to free your creative spirit. It is a beginning, a first step on the long path. Creativity is a never-ending process that continues all around us and manifests itself within us. It lies at the deepest core of our being and at the universe's deepest heart.

Creativity comes from doing what must be done: from expressing the creative spirit within us and not allowing it to be silenced. We do and must create. Creativity is not for the faint-hearted, but it is for those who are prepared to take responsibility for themselves and for the Divine spirit of creativity within them. This can be daunting. Creative people take risks by committing themselves to creative work, which may be relinquishing other, safer, career paths. They take risks by voicing, expressing, and creating new forms and modes of artistic expression; by exploring their being and finding ways for this to be expressed. Creative risks are about saying; "I will try to do this. I may fail, but trying will be fun." Creativity is a Divine gift. It is the true essence of our very selves—and what is the point of a life opportunity wasted, of talent unexpressed, and life unlived?

Let us make of our lives a creative work, of joy, beauty, pain, sorrow, and above all of aspiration—the courage to take the great leap forward and to reach for the stars.

In Indian Tantric teaching, the goddess Shakti is *prakrti*, the active principle of the universe. Shakti is creative energy, but energy alone does not produce creativity. Energy must be channeled into form. In Tantra, form is represented by the god Shiva. In our own creative process, we must have both force and form. We need energy and ideas, as well as the technical skills that turn them into form—image, word, movement, or sound. To be creative, we must be willing to listen to the voice of creativity within the universe. For some people this is God, for others Goddess, for some the force of life itself. Whatever our spiritual beliefs, as creative people we can see that our universe is purposeful and seeks to manifest itself in all the myriad and wondrous forms that it can. As

> 66 But we must not forget that only a few people are artists in life; that the art of life is the most distinguished and rarest of all the arts. 99
>
> CARL GUSTAV JUNG, *psychotherapist*

creators, we become instruments for the creative forces of the universe. We become at one with the gods and we seek to do the greater will of the universe. As instruments of the universe, we draw close to the collective unconscious, the collective psyche of humankind. We dive into its depths and draw upon many commonalties, those symbols, archetypes, inspirations, and ideas that take us beyond our own experience, to become manifesters of ideas and images that speak to the societies of which we are members. We transcend our boundaries and access the group mind of us all. We become the eyes, ears, hands, and brains of creative deity. Let us listen, then, to the voice of the Creatrix. Let us seek the creative power—*Satchitananda, Being–Consciousness–Bliss*—and unite ourselves with our Divine source: that which gave birth to us and that to which we all return.

Voice of the Creatrix

I am thy Goddess;
   high born, full-blooded and lusting free am I;
   the wind is my voice and my song.
   High and low,
   breeze and whirlwind,
   soft and sweet,
   loud and shrill,
   wild is my will,
   and impetuous my desire.

  I take whom I will;
    no one can refuse my love and live.
   And those to whom I have revealed myself,
  are the blessed of women and men.
   They have won the favor of the High Gods,
  and who shall refuse the behest of the Gods;
 for you are but leaves,
blown upon the wind.

I am thy Goddess;
before the beginning of time was I.
I made the mountains into peaks,
 and laid with soft grass the valleys and the meadows.
Mine was the first foot that trod upon the Earth,
and where I walked there sprung forth flowers,
and mine was the voice that gave rise to the first song,
and the birds listened and heard and made return.
In the dawn of the world, I taught the sea its song,
and mine were the tears that made the first rains.

Listen and hear me;
    for none can escape me.
    It was I who gave birth to you,
    and in the depths of my earth,
    you will find rest and rebirth,
    and I will spring you forth anew,
    a fresh shoot to greenness.

    Fear me,
   love me,
   adore me,
  lose yourself in me.
I am the wine of life,
I stir the senses,
I put song in the heart and on the lips of men;
before the battle I give my strength,
I am the Creative Power.

VIVIANNE CROWLEY

remember

- Being creative is holistic: it involves all aspects of ourselves.

- Being in tune with one's body through meditation and relaxation encourages the flow of creativity.

- Creativity is an alchemical process: it combines earth, water, fire, and air.

- The fifth alchemical element is spirit, represented by alchemical gold. Creativity is the gateway to spirit.

- A final thing to remember: you are a creator and your life is your song.

Singing the song, I rejoice.

Bibliography

ADAMS, DOUGLAS, *The Hitch-Hiker's Guide to the Galaxy*,
New York, Ballantine Books: 1995

ALBERS, JOSEPH, *Interaction of Color*, New Haven and London,
Yale University Press: 1963

BACHOFEN, J.J., *Myth, Religion, and Mother-Right*, Princeton,
Princeton University Press: 1861

BOHM, DAVID, *On Creativity*, LEE NICHOL (ed.),
London, Routledge:1998

CAMPBELL, JOSEPH, *The Hero with a Thousand Faces*, Bollingen Series
XVII, Princeton, Princeton University Press: 1972

CAMUS, ALBERT, *The Plague*, New York, Vintage Books: 1991

ELBOW, PETER, *Writing with Power: Techniques for Mastering the
Writing Process*, Oxford, Oxford University Press: 1981

—*Writing Without Teachers*, Oxford,
Oxford University Press: 1973

HINE, PHIL, *Walking Between the Worlds: Techniques of Modern
Shamanism*, Vol. 1, Leeds, Pagan News Publications: 1989

ITTEN, JOHANNES, *The Elements of Color: A Treatise on the Color
System of Johannes Itten*, FABER BIRREN (ed.), ERNST VAN HAGEN
(trans.), New York, Wiley and Sons: 1970

JEFFERS, SUSAN, *Feel the Fear and Do it Anyway*,
London, Arrow: 1996

JUNG, CARL G., *The Collected Works of C.G. Jung,
Vol. 5, Symbols of Transformation*,
London, Routledge, & Kegan Paul: 1967

MAY, ROLLO, *The Courage to Create*, New York,
W.W. Norton & Company: 1994

MICHELS, CAROLL, *How to Survive and Prosper as an Artist:
Selling Yourself Without Selling Your Soul*,
New York, Henry Holt: 1997

MORRIS, WILLIAM, *Hopes and Fears for Art*,
London, Ellis and White: 1882

MURRAY, W.H., *The Scottish Himalayan Expedition*,
London, J.M. Dent & Sons: 1951

PROUST, MARCEL, *Swann's Way: The Remembrance of Things Past*,
Vol. 1, London, Penguin: 1998

ROBERTS, ROYSTON M., *Serendipity, Accidental Discoveries in Science*,
New York, John Wiley and Sons: 1989

STERMBERG, ROBERT J., *Handbook of Creativity*,
Cambridge, Cambridge University Press: 1999

WALLAS, GRAHAM, *The Art of Thought*, New York, Harcourt: 1926

WELTY, EUDORA, *One Writer's Beginnings*,
Cambridge, Mass, Harvard University Press: 1986

index